Introduction to Applied Phonetics
Laboratory Workbook

Introduction
to
Applied Phonetics

Laboratory Workbook

by
Mary Louise Edwards, Ph.D.
Syracuse University

COLLEGE-HILL PRESS, San Diego, California

College-Hill Press, Inc.
4284 41st Street
San Diego, California 92105

© 1986 College-Hill Press, Inc.

ISBN 0-88744-128-9

Printed in the United States of America

To my phonetics teachers—

Ilse Lehiste
Clara N. Bush

CONTENTS

PREFACE

This workbook and the accompanying audio cassette tapes were developed to help students in communication disorders and linguistics learn basic phonetic transcription. They were designed to be used in an introductory phonetics course. The workbook is not intended to serve as a basic text, but rather to reinforce relevant course content and to provide students with transcription practice.

These materials constitute seven laboratory sessions and three laboratory reviews covering oral and nasal stop consonants, fricatives and affricates, liquids and glides, front and back vowels, central vowels and diphthongs, commonly used diacritics, and suprasegmentals. The laboratory sessions were designed to give students experience with broad transcription of specific classes of sounds before expecting them to deal with diacritics or to handle several classes of sounds at once. Because students just beginning to learn phonetics often feel that they are expected to do "too much too soon," an attempt was made to break the task of phonetic transcription into small steps and to sequence the practice exercises so that they would gradually increase in difficulty. Although the laboratory sessions were planned to fit into the structure of an introductory phonetics course, they were also designed to be completed by students working independently, at their own pace in a listening laboratory.

For each laboratory session, specific objectives are listed; students are told what they are expected to be able to do by the end of the session. For sounds within real words, they are generally expected to reach a level of 95% accuracy and for the same sounds within made-up (nonsense) words, 90% accuracy is usually required.

After a review of relevant content (e.g., concerning the production of oral stop consonants) and the necessary phonetic symbols, examples are given to illustrate the production of the sounds covered in the laboratory in various positions within real words. (Initial, medial, and final positions are included, along with clusters.)

Next there is a self-test that contains both real and nonsense words. This test allows students to gauge how much they already know about the content of the laboratory session. Students check their own answers, and, depending on their scores, they may skip over most of the practice exercises in the laboratory or may be asked to complete all of the exercises.

The practice exercises (approximately seven) in each laboratory session are graded in difficulty, with the first (discrimination) exercise being the easiest. To control the level of difficulty, several parameters were manipulated. As a result, some exercises involve only hearing the word *(aural only presentation)* and transcribing sounds in particular word positions or in all positions. Other exercises involve *written and aural presentation* and require listening for the target sounds in a variety of positions. Each laboratory session contains some exercises that involve nonsense words. These were included to give students experience in listening for familiar sounds in unfamiliar sequences and to partially simulate the transcription of disordered or foreign speech. Most laboratory sessions also include a *sagittal sections* exercise, in which students are given schematic diagrams representing various places and manners of articulation and are asked to match the sound they hear with the appropriate diagram.

At the end of each laboratory session is a test, made up of both real and nonsense words. (The answers to these tests are not included in the workbook but are available in a separate booklet.) The test is the only part of each laboratory session that students are required to hand in. If all practice exercises have been completed, students should achieve the desired level of accuracy on the test. However, if a student does not reach the expected level, it is recommended that the instructor provide appropriate remedial exercises (not included here) or have the student repeat selected exercises within the laboratory.

There are three laboratory reviews in this workbook that give students an opportunity to piece together what they have learned. For instance, after learning to transcribe oral and nasal stops (Laboratory Session 1), fricatives and affricates (Laboratory Session 2), and liquid and glides (Laboratory Session 3), there is a laboratory review covering all of the consonants of English.

Because these laboratory sessions are self-paced, each one may be completed very quickly or may take one or two hours, depending on the prior knowledge and experience of the student and on his or her aptitude for phonetic transcription. (In addition, the laboratory sessions differ somewhat in the number of sounds covered and in the number of practice exercises included. For example, Laboratory Session 1, which covers nine sounds and which was planned to acquaint students with transcription, is quite lengthy.) Average times are listed for each laboratory session, based on the experience of the students using the materials in 1983 and 1984.

Although these materials were designed to accompany a lecture course, they may also be used by students working on their own, who wish to brush up on their phonetic transcription skills or who wish to review the content of an earlier course in applied phonetics.

It is hoped that instructors will find these materials to be as helpful and effective as I have found them to be with my own classes. Because they do not cover everything, it may be necessary to supplement them, depending on the scope of the course for which they are used. For example, they deal only with the transcription of single words, and there is only one session (Laboratory Session 6) that deals with diacritics. It serves to introduce students to narrow transcription and to familiarize them with some commonly used diacritics, but there are many diacritics that are not covered, and students will need much more practice than is provided in Laboratory Session 6 to master narrow transcription. (A list of additional symbols and diacritics can be found in the appendix.) Students also need exposure to disordered or foreign speech. However, these topics are beyond the scope of this book. (Shriberg and Kent, 1982, provide practice with the transcription of disordered speech, and materials by Smalley, 1963, provide both transcription and production practice with sounds that do not occur in English.)

Laboratory Session 7, which deals with suprasegmentals, is also rather limited, covering only word stress, intonation, and (to a very small extent) length. Tone, which is not a feature of English, is not covered at all, and juncture and rhythm are not included. The system that is presented for transcribing intonation (based on that of Grate, 1974) is only one of many possible alternatives. For example, a very different system was presented by George Allen at the 1984 convention of the American Speech-Language-Hearing Association.

I am grateful to many people for their assistance in the development and preparation of this workbook and the accompanying audiotapes. First, I must express my gratitude to the Lilly Endowment, Inc. This project might never have been undertaken had I not received a Postdoctoral Teaching Award from the Lilly Endowment.

Second, I would like to express my sincere thanks to the staff members of the Center for Instructional Development at Syracuse University. In particular, Barbara Petry, John Konarski, and Robin Taylor were extremely helpful during various phases of this project. Martha Strain, who prepared the illustrations found throughout this book, also deserves thanks, as does June Mermigos for her many hours of word processing.

Third, my warm appreciation goes to Professor Patricia Moody, who graciously agreed to serve as my Lilly Project Mentor and who offered invaluable assistance throughout the preparation of these materials.

Thanks are also extended to the staff of Audio Services at Syracuse University and to the classes of students in applied phonetics who took the time to evaluate each laboratory session and whose feedback was essential in the modification and refinement of the laboratory workbook and the audiotapes.

Connie Salvetti and Lena Rose Orlando are also to be thanked for their help in typing the manuscript.

Finally, sincere appreciation to the staff at College-Hill Press for their advice and assistance.

Note to Students and General Instructions for Using This Workbook and Accompanying Audiotapes

NOTE TO STUDENTS

One of the most important skills that you are expected to learn in your phonetics course is how to transcribe speech using the phonetic alphabet. Phonetic transcription is an essential skill for students in communication disorders and linguistics, as well as in various other disciplines. However, it is a skill that takes a great deal of practice to develop. In fact, practice is the key to learning and feeling comfortable with phonetic transcription. The laboratory exercises contained in this workbook and the accompanying audiotapes were designed to give you this essential practice. It is hoped that you will find them useful and enjoyable.

Read the following instructions and guidelines before going to the laboratory, and refer to them whenever necessary.

GENERAL INSTRUCTIONS:

1. Seven laboratory sessions and three laboratory reviews are included in this workbook. For each laboratory session, there is just one assignment (a test) to hand in. Your instructor will tell you when each laboratory test is due. All the forms you will need are included here.
2. Each laboratory lesson begins with a statement of the objectives and a review of the content and relevant phonetic symbols. Read these parts over to yourself. Do not turn on the tape recorder until you are told to do so. Toward the beginning of each laboratory session is a "self-test." If you do very well on the self-test, you may skip some of the laboratory exercises. Otherwise, you will be expected to complete all of the exercises.
3. The material in each laboratory session is graded in difficulty, with the last exercises being the most difficult. You may work at your own pace in completing each laboratory session. You will notice that made-up (nonsense) words are included to give you experience in hearing familiar sounds in unfamiliar sequences. Because nonsense words tend to be more difficult to transcribe than real words, they are graded more leniently.

4. Each word, real or made-up, that you are to listen to is said twice, with a two or three second pause between presentations. In many cases, this should give you enough time to do what is required. If you need to stop the tape to think about a sound or phonetic symbol, feel free to do so. If you need to hear a word a third or fourth time, rewind the tape slightly and play that part of the tape over again. However, try to do what is required without rewinding the tape. Later on, when you are asked to transcribe "live" (i.e., without a tape recording), you will not be able to ask the speaker to repeat each word many times. Two productions should generally be sufficient.

5. After each exercise, or occasionally after two or three exercises, you will be told to stop the tape and check your answers. The answers for each practice exercise are given in the back of the workbook.

6. You should aim for 95% accuracy in your transcriptions. In some cases, you may need to repeat an exercise to attain this level of accuracy. You will be told when to go on to the next exercise. Although this may seem to be a very stringent requirement, it is necessary because a phonetic transcription must be highly accurate to be useful.

7. Please note that the laboratory sessions differ somewhat in format, depending on which sounds (and how many sounds) are covered. They also differ in length, again partly because of the nature of their content. Thus, it is not possible to predict how long it will take you to complete these laboratory sessions. In addition, because everyone will be working at his or her own pace, the amount of time spent on any one session will vary. However, on the page with the objectives an average time is given, along with a range, based on past students' shortest and longest times reported for the laboratory.

8. Take a short break after transcribing for approximately 30 to 45 minutes. Turn off the playback machine, take off the headphones, and stretch. Because phonetic transcription requires a lot of concentration, it is important to take frequent breaks.

Laboratory Session 1
Oral and Nasal Stop Consonants

OBJECTIVES

In this laboratory session you will learn to recognize and to transcribe oral and nasal stop consonants in a variety of positions in both real and nonsense words. By the end of this session, you will be expected to meet two specific objectives:

- First, when presented with a spoken list of 15 real words containing oral and nasal stop consonants in a variety of word positions, you will correctly transcribe the oral and nasal stops with 95% accuracy (without visual cues).
- Second, while listening to 10 nonsense words containing oral and nasal stop consonants in a variety of positions, you will correctly transcribe those consonants with 90% accuracy.

AVERAGE TIME

1 ½ hours (range: 40 minutes to 2³/₄ hours)

NOTE: This laboratory session consists of two parts: Part A (oral stop consonants) and Part B (nasal stop consonants). Because this is a long laboratory session, you may want to do the two parts separately. However, the test at the end covers both parts of the laboratory, so you will want to review Part A before taking the test.

PART A

ORAL STOP CONSONANTS

I.   Review of Content: Oral Stop Consonants

English has six oral stop consonants. Three of them are *voiceless;* that is, they are produced without vibration of the vocal folds. These three sounds are /p/, /t/, and /k/. The corresponding *voiced* stops, produced with vibration of the vocal folds, are /b/, /d/, and /g/.

Table 1 contains the symbols representing the six oral stop consonants of English and shows the place of articulation and voicing quality of each one.

Table 1.   Oral Stop Consonants of English

		Place of Articulation		
		Bilabial	Alveolar	Velar
Voicing	−	p	t	k
	+	b	d	g

Oral stop consonants are produced with total obstruction or closure at some point in the mouth. If the obstruction involves the upper and lower lips, a *bilabial* stop is produced. This is shown in Figure 1. /p/ and /b/, as in *Paul* and *ball,* are voiceless and voiced bilabial stops, respectively.

If the closure involves the tip or blade of the tongue and the alveolar ridge, an *alveolar* stop is produced. This is illustrated in Figure 2. /t/ and /d/, as in *tip* and *dip,* are voiceless and voiced alveolar stops.

If the closure involves the back (dorsum) of the tongue and the soft palate (velum), a *velar* stop is produced, as shown in Figure 3. /k/ and /g/ as in *coat* and *goat,* are the voiceless and voiced velar stops.

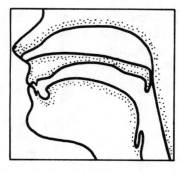

Figure 1

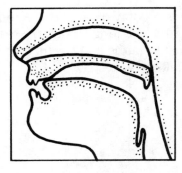

Figure 2

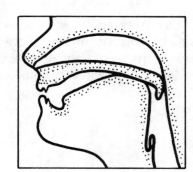

Figure 3

II. Examples

The examples that follow illustrate the production of oral stop consonants in various positions within words and in the context of various vowels and consonants.* You will notice that oral stop consonants sound somewhat different depending on the position in which they occur and depending on the surrounding sounds. For now, do not worry about these differences. Later on, you will learn how to capture them in your transcriptions.

Turn on the tape recorder and follow along.

	Initial	Final	Medial	Clusters
/p/	peaceful	deep	napkin	priceless
	poor	elope	upper	kept
	putter	recoup	repeal	lapsed
			stickpin	sprain
/b/	barren	crib	maybe	blender
	button	club	lobster	bronze
	boot	jab	embassy	sobbed
			absent	garb
/t/	telephone	repeat	blister	tremble
	thyme	hurt	empty	store
	tomato	caught	batman	parts
			baton	belt
/d/	daily	feed	payday	drain
	daring	pawed	badly	held
	durable	repaid	leader	yards
			meddle	land
/k/	king	steak	napkin	clipper
	carriage	book	taxi	squid
	caught	hemlock	macaroni	box
			monkey	picked
/g/	geese	beg	alligator	grain
	gallon	smog	arrogant	Gwendolyn
	gully	rogue	igloo	icebergs
			iguana	pigs

*The four positions of concern in all of the laboratory sessions in this book are defined as follows: *initial*—a singleton consonant that initiates a word; *final*—a singleton consonant that terminates a word; *medial*—a consonant that occurs within a word, that is, not at the beginning or the end; *cluster*—a sequence of two or more consonants together in the same syllable.

III. Self-Test: Oral Stop Consonants

This self-test will assess your ability to recognize and transcribe oral stop consonants in real and nonsense words. It will also give you an indication of what you will need to be able to do by the end of this part of Laboratory Session 1 (on oral stop consonants).

In the spaces provided, write the correct symbols for the oral stop consonants contained in the real words and nonsense words that will now be heard.

Start tape now.

Real words

1. _____ _____   6. _____   _____   _____   _____
2. _____ _____   7 _____   _____
3. _____ _____   8. _____   _____
4. _____ _____   9. _____   _____   _____
5. _____ _____ _____   10. _____   _____

Nonsense words

11. _____ _____ _____   15. _____   _____   _____
12. _____ _____   16. _____   _____   _____
13. _____ _____ _____   17. _____   _____
14. _____ _____   18. _____   _____   _____

To see how well you did on this self-test, check the answers in the back of this workbook.

- If you made 0 to 2 errors, go directly to exercise F. However, you may wish to do some of the earlier exercises for additional practice.
- If you made more than 2 errors, you will need to do all of the exercises for oral stop consonants.

IV. Practice Exercises

The following exercises are graded in difficulty. That is, the last ones will be the hardest. Work at your own pace and write your answers in the appropriate spaces.

A. Yes-No Discriminations

You will now hear 12 short syllables, each of which contains one consonant sound. For each syllable, indicate whether or not the consonant is an *oral stop*. If it is, check the plus (+) column; if it is not, check the (−) column.

Start tape now.

	+	−		+	−
1.			7.		
2.			8.		
3.			9.		
4.			10.		
5.			11.		
6.			12.		

For each nonsense word that will now be heard, check the correct column to indicate whether or not there is a *voiced oral stop*.

	+	−		+	−
13.			18.		
14.			19.		
15.			20.		
16.			21.		
17.			22.		

Indicate whether or not each nonsense word that will now be heard contains a *velar stop*.

	+	−		+	−
23.			27.		
24.			28.		
25.			29.		
26.			30.		

Check your answers in the back of this workbook. If you missed more than 1 item, repeat this exercise, paying close attention to the items with which you had difficulty. If you missed 0 or 1 item, go to the next page.

B. Aural Only Presentation: Specific Positions

The lists of words that will now be presented contain oral stop consonants in specified positions. In each case, write the correct symbol for the stop that you hear in the space provided.

Start tape now.

Initial position

1. _____	7. _____
2. _____	8. _____
3. _____	9. _____
4. _____	10. _____
5. _____	11. _____
6. _____	12. _____

Initial clusters

37. _____	43. _____
38. _____	44. _____
39. _____	45. _____
40. _____	46. _____
41. _____	47. _____
42. _____	48. _____

Final position

13. _____	19. _____
14. _____	20. _____
15. _____	21. _____
16. _____	22. _____
17. _____	23. _____
18. _____	24. _____

Final clusters

49. _____	55. _____
50. _____	56. _____
51. _____	57. _____
52. _____	58. _____
53. _____	59. _____
54. _____	60. _____

Medial position

25. _____	31. _____
26. _____	32. _____
27. _____	33. _____
28. _____	34. _____
29. _____	35. _____
30. _____	36. _____

Check your answers in the back of this workbook. If you made 3 or more errors, you should go back and repeat this lesson. Start with the review of content or with the examples given earlier, and pay particular attention to the sounds that were a problem for you. If 0 to 2 errors, go on.

C. Written and Aural Presentation: Combined Positions

The words in the following list contain oral stop consonants in a variety of word positions and phonetic contexts. In the space provided, write the correct symbol for the one oral stop contained in each word.

Start tape now.

1.	_____	tongue	13.	_____	pouring
2.	_____	empathy	14.	_____	finger
3.	_____	conjure	15.	_____	fired
4.	_____	earlobe	16.	_____	slope
5.	_____	relevant	17.	_____	cling
6.	_____	dough	18.	_____	master
7.	_____	fugue	19.	_____	absolve
8.	_____	flick	20.	_____	glower
9.	_____	banish	21.	_____	princely
10.	_____	driver	22.	_____	modern
11.	_____	axis	23.	_____	fought
12.	_____	garnish	24.	_____	blemish

Check your answers for this exercise in the back of the book. If you made more than 1 error, please repeat this exercise. If you made 0 or 1 error, go on to the next exercise.

D. Aural Only Presentation: Combined Positions—Real Words

The words that you will now hear contain oral stop consonants in various positions. In the space provided, write the correct symbol for the oral stop consonant contained in each word.

Start tape now.

1.	_____	10.	_____
2.	_____	11.	_____
3.	_____	12.	_____
4.	_____	13.	_____
5.	_____	14.	_____
6.	_____	15.	_____
7.	_____	16.	_____
8.	_____	17.	_____
9.	_____	18.	_____

E. Aural Only Presentation: Combined Positions—Nonsense Words

Each nonsense word that will now be heard contains one oral stop consonant. The position in which the stop is found varies from word to word. In the space provided, write the appropriate symbol for the stop contained in each nonsense word.

Start tape now.

1. _____   7. _____
2. _____   8. _____
3. _____   9. _____
4. _____   10. _____
5. _____   11. _____
6. _____   12. _____

Check your answers for these exercises in the back of this book. If you made more than 1 error, please repeat the exercise. If you made 0 to 1 error, go on to the next exercise.

F. Sagittal Sections

Each word that will now be heard contains one oral stop consonant. Identify the place of articulation of the stop by writing the letter of the appropriate sagittal section (a, b, or c) in the space provided.

Start tape now.

1. _____   7. _____
2. _____   8. _____
3. _____   9. _____
4. _____   10. _____
5. _____   11. _____
6. _____   12. _____

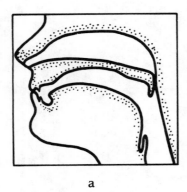   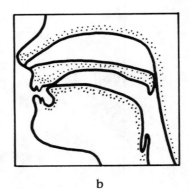   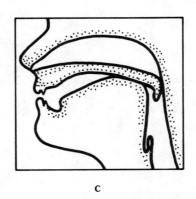

  a   b   c

Look at the answers in the back of the book to see if you made any errors. If you did, you should repeat the exercise. If you made no errors, good job! Go on to Exercise G.

G. Final Exercise: Oral Stops

In the spaces provided, write the correct symbols for the oral stops contained in the words that will now be heard. In each case, the correct number of spaces is given.

Start tape now.

Real words

1. _____ _____   6. _____ _____

2. _____ _____   7. _____ _____

3. _____ _____   8. _____ _____

4. _____ _____ _____   9. _____ _____

5. _____ _____ _____   10. _____ _____

Nonsense words

11. _____ _____ _____   15. _____ _____ _____

12. _____ _____ _____   16. _____ _____ _____

13. _____ _____ _____   17. _____ _____

14. _____ _____ _____

Check your answers in the back of this workbook. If you missed more than 2 symbols on this exercise, go back and listen again to the review of content and the examples given at the beginning of this laboratory session. Then redo this exercise. If you made 0 to 2 errors, congratulations! You are ready to go on to Part B of this laboratory session. You may continue with the session now or do Part B at a later time.

PART B

NASAL STOP CONSONANTS

I. Review of Content: Nasal Stops

English has three nasal stop consonants—one bilabial, one alveolar, and one velar. So, they are produced at the same points in the mouth as are oral stops. Like oral stops, they involve complete closure between two articulators, but there is no velopharynegal closure during their production. Thus, air can flow into the nasal cavity. Unlike oral stops, all nasal stops are voiced; they do not occur in voiceless-voiced pairs. The symbols for the nasal stops are shown in Table 2.

Table 2. Nasal Stop Consonants of English

Place of Articulation		
Bilabial	Alveolar	Velar
m	n	ŋ

Figures 4, 5, and 6 show the position of the articulators during the production of the bilabial nasal /m/, the alveolar nasal /n/, and the velar nasal /ŋ/, respectively. Note that the velopharyngeal port is open.

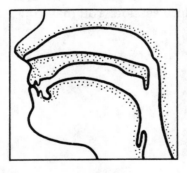 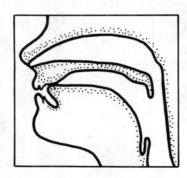 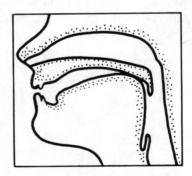

Figure 4   Figure 5   Figure 6

II. Examples

The examples that follow illustrate the production of nasal stops in various positions within words and in the context of various vowels and consonants.

Turn on tape recorder and follow along.

	Initial	*Final*	*Medial*	*Clusters*
/m/	movie	fame	lemon	farm
	machine	thumb	damage	smoke
	magnificent	bedlam	limber	slammed
				lambs
/n/	naughty	alone	danger	tense
	pneumonia	reason	canister	warrant
	gnat	champagne	sandy	fanned
			banana	snake
/ŋ/	—	bring	monkey	think
		sitting	singer	plank
		belong	jungle	songs
			linger	banged

III. Self-Test: Nasal Stop Consonants

This self-test will assess your ability to recognize and transcribe nasal stops in real and nonsense words. Also, it will give you an indication of what you will need to be able to do by the end of this part of Laboratory Session 1 (on nasal stop consonants).

In the spaces provided, write the correct symbols for the nasal stop consonants contained in the real and nonsense words that will now be heard.

Start tape now.

Real words

1. _____   _____   6. _____   _____
2. _____   _____   7. _____   _____
3. _____   _____   8. _____   _____
4. _____   _____   9. _____
5. _____   _____   10. _____   _____   _____

Nonsense words

11. _____   _____   15. _____   _____
12. _____   _____   16. _____   _____
13. _____   _____   17. _____   _____
14. _____   _____   18. _____   _____

Check your answers in the back of this workbook.

- If you made 0 to 2 errors, go directly to Exercise F in Part IV (Practice Exercises). However, you may wish to do some of the earlier exercises (A–E) for additional practice.
- If you made more than 2 errors, you will need to do all the practice exercises in Part IV of this laboratory session.

IV. Practice Exercises

The following exercises are graded in difficulty. That is, the last ones will be the hardest. Work at your own pace. Write your answers in the appropriate spaces.

A. Yes–No Discriminations

You will now hear 12 nonsense words. For each one, indicate in the space provided whether or not the word contains a nasal stop. If it does, check the plus (+) column. If not, check the minus (−) column.

Start tape now.

	+	−		+	−
1.	_____	_____	7.	_____	_____
2.	_____	_____	8.	_____	_____
3.	_____	_____	9.	_____	_____
4.	_____	_____	10.	_____	_____
5.	_____	_____	11.	_____	_____
6.	_____	_____	12.	_____	_____

When you are finished with this first exercise, check your answers in the back of this workbook. If you missed any items, repeat the exercise, paying close attention to the items that gave you difficulty. If you made no errors, go on to Exercise B.

B. Aural Only Presentation: Specific Positions

The lists of words that will now be presented contain nasal stop consonants in specified positions. In each case, write the correct symbol for the nasal stop that you hear in the space provided.

Start tape now.

Initial position   *Medial position*

1. _____   4. _____   16. _____   19. _____

2. _____   5. _____   17. _____   20. _____

3. _____   6. _____   18. _____   21. _____

Final position   *Clusters*

7. _____   12. _____   22. _____   26. _____

8. _____   13. _____   23. _____   27. _____

9. _____   14. _____   24. _____   28. _____

10. _____   15. _____   25. _____

11. _____

Now look in the back of this workbook to check your answers on this section. If you made more than 1 error, go back and repeat this exercise. You may want to start with the review of content or with the examples given earlier. Pay particular attention to the sounds that were a problem for you. If you made 0 or 1 error, go on to Exercise C.

C. Written and Aural Presentation: Combined Positions

The words in the following list contain nasal stops in a variety of word positions and phonetic contexts. In the space provided write the appropriate symbol for the one nasal stop contained in each word.

Start tape now.

1. _____   gnaw   6. _____   camped

2. _____   finger   7. _____   sandwich

3. _____   limber   8. _____   marriage

4. _____   hinge   9. _____   sink

5. _____   fitting

Go on to the next exercise.

D. Aural Only Presentation: Combined Positions—Real Words

In the space provided, write the appropriate symbol for the nasal stop contained in each word.

Start tape now.

1. _____   4. _____

2. _____   5. _____

3. _____   6. _____

E. Aural Only Presentation: Combined Positions—Nonsense Words

Each nonsense word that will be heard contains one nasal stop consonant. In the space provided, write the correct symbol for the nasal stop in each nonsense word.

Start tape now.

1. _____   4. _____

2. _____   5. _____

3. _____   6. _____

Check your answers for these exercises by looking in the back of the book. If you made more than 1 error, please repeat the exercises that gave you difficulty. Otherwise, go on to Exercise F.

F. Sagittal Sections

Each word that will now be heard contains one nasal stop. Identify the place of articulation of the nasal stop (bilabial, alveolar, or velar) and write the letter of the correct diagram (sagittal section) in the space provided.

Start tape now.

1. _____   4. _____

2. _____   5. _____

3. _____   6. _____

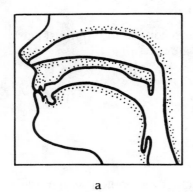 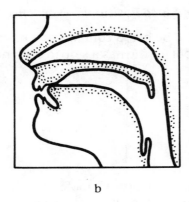 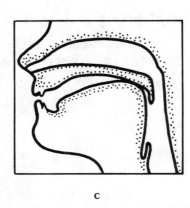

a   b   c

Look at the answers to see if you made any errors. If you did, please repeat this exercise. If you made none, good job! Go on to Exercise G.

G. Final Exercise: Nasal Stops

In the spaces provided, write the correct symbols for the nasal stop consonants in the words that will now be heard. In each case, the correct number of spaces is given.

Start tape now.

Real words

1. _____ _____   5. _____

2. _____ _____ _____   6. _____   _____

3. _____   7. _____

4. _____   8. _____   _____

Nonsense words

9. _____ _____   12. _____   _____

10. _____ _____   13. _____

11. _____ _____   14. _____   _____

Check your answers to this exercise by looking in the back of this workbook. If you missed more than one symbol, you should go back to the review of content and the examples given at the beginning of the nasal stop portion of this session. Then redo this final exercise. If you made fewer than 2 errors, congratulations! You are ready to go on to the test for this laboratory session. Remember that you may need to go back and review the first section (on oral stops) before taking the test.

TEST: ORAL AND NASAL STOP CONSONANTS

In the spaces provided, write the correct symbols for the oral and nasal stop consonants contained in the words that will now be heard. To pass this test and the laboratory session, you will need to make fewer than 3 errors on the real words and fewer than 4 errors on the nonsense words.

Start tape now.

Real words

1. _____ _____   9. _____ _____

2. _____ _____   10. _____ _____ _____

3. _____ _____ _____ _____   11. _____ _____

4. _____ _____   12. _____ _____ _____

5. _____ _____   13. _____ _____

6. _____ _____ _____   14. _____ _____

7. _____ _____ _____ _____   15. _____ _____

8. _____ _____

Nonsense words

16. _____ _____   21. _____ _____ _____ _____

17. _____ _____   22. _____ _____ _____ _____

18. _____ _____ _____   23. _____ _____ _____

19. _____ _____ _____   24. _____ _____ _____

20. _____ _____ _____   25. _____ _____ _____

Laboratory Session 2
Fricatives and Affricates

OBJECTIVES

In this laboratory session you will learn to recognize and to transcribe fricative and affricate consonants in a variety of positions in both real and nonsense (made-up) words. By the end of this session, you will be expected to meet two specific objectives:

- First, when presented with a spoken list of 15 real words containing fricatives and affricates in a variety of positions, you will correctly transcribe the fricatives and affricates in those words with 90% accuracy (without visual cues).
- Second, while listening to 10 nonsense words containing fricatives and affricates in a variety of positions, you will correctly transcribe those consonants with 90% accuracy.

AVERAGE TIME

1 1/2 hours (range: 45 minutes to 2 3/4 hours)

FRICATIVES

I.   Review of Content

English has eight fricatives or spirants. Four of them are voiceless; that is, they are produced without vibration of the vocal folds. These four fricatives are /θ/, /f/, /s/, and /ʃ/. (/h/, which is sometimes considered a fricative, is also voiceless.) The corresponding voiced fricatives, produced with vibration of the vocal folds, are /ð/, /v/, /z/, and /ʒ/.

Fricatives are produced with narrowing or constriction at some point in the vocal tract sufficient to create friction or turbulence in the airstream, but there is no complete closure. If the constriction involves the tip or blade of the tongue between the upper and lower teeth (or slightly behind the upper teeth), an interdental fricative is produced. This is shown in Figure 7. /θ/ and /ð/, as in *thin* and *then,* are the voiceless and voiced interdental fricatives, respectively.

If the constriction involves the upper teeth being held lightly against the bottom lip, a labiodental fricative is produced. This is shown in Figure 8. /f/ and /v/, as in *fail* and *veil,* are the voiceless and voiced labiodental fricatives, respectively.

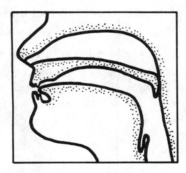

Figure 7

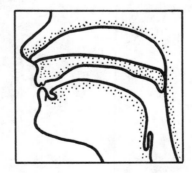

Figure 8

If the constriction involves the tip or blade of the tongue and the alveolar ridge, an alveolar fricative is produced. This is shown in Figure 9. /s/ and /z/, as in *Sue* and *zoo,* are the voiceless and voiced alveolar fricatives, respectively.

If there is constriction between the blade of the tongue and the postalveolar or prepalatal region of the mouth, a palato-alveolar or alveolo-palatal fricative is produced. This is shown in Figure 10. /ʃ/ and /ʒ/, as in *pressure* and *pleasure,* are the voiceless and voiced palato-alveolar fricatives, respectively. These sounds are usually called simply palatal fricatives. For all fricatives, the velopharyngeal port is closed.

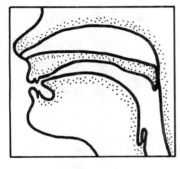

Figure 9

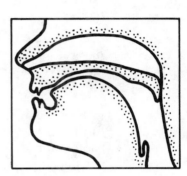

Figure 10

The constriction involved in the production of /h/ is at the glottis. Therefore, /h/ is sometimes considered to be a voiceless glottal fricative.

Four of the fricatives of English are called "hissing" fricatives or *sibilants* because they are produced with more high frequency energy. These sounds are /s/, /z/, /ʃ/, and /ʒ/.

Table 3 contains the phonetic symbols for the fricative consonants of English and shows the place of articulation and the voicing quality of each one.

Table 3.   Fricative Consonants of English

		Place of Articulation			
Voicing	Interdental	Labiodental	Alveolar	Palato-Alveolar	Glottal
−	θ	f	s	ʃ	h
+	ð	v	z	ʒ	

II. Examples: Fricatives

The examples that follow illustrate the production of fricative consonants in various positions within words and in the context of various consonants and vowels.

Start tape now.

	Initial	*Final*	*Medial*	*Clusters*
/θ/	thumb	teeth	healthy	three
	thimble	mouth	ether	hearth
	thought	beneath	birthday	health
			toothbrush	tenth
/ð/	these	breathe	neither	lathes
	them	writhe	further	breathes
		wreathe	earthenware	mouthed
			rather	writhed
/f/	furnish	giraffe	after	flower
	photograph	cough	laughter	phrase
	philately	half	coffee	elf
			careful	scarf
/v/	vest	glove	oven	wives
	vanquish	remove	lovely	elves
	volleyball	beehive	seventeen	curved
			mover	behaved
/s/	scent	voice	rooster	spring
	century	loose	gasoline	collapse
	pseudonym	embrace	faces	tense
			taxi	vex
/z/	zebra	lose	razor	dazed
	zipper	maze	scissors	amused
	xylophone	owes	paisley	adz
			busy	legs
/ʃ/	shelter	dish	washing	shrimp
	chute	leash	mission	schmaltz
	sharing	smash	ashen	marsh
			fissure	cashed
/ʒ/	genre	beige	vision	
		rouge	measure	
		barrage	leisure	
		mirage		
/h/	hay		ahead	
	heavenly		doghouse	
	hamburger		icehouse	
	help		behind	

AFFRICATES

I. Review of Content

English has just two affricates, a voiceless-voiced pair produced at the palato-alveolar or alveolo-palatal region of the mouth. (They are usually referred to simply as "palatal.") Affricates begin like stops—with complete closure between two articulators—but instead of being released abruptly, as stops are, they are released gradually, with frication. So, they begin like stops and end like fricatives. This is shown in the diagrams below (Figures 11a and 11b). /tʃ/ and /dʒ/, as in *chin* and *gin*, are the voiceless and voiced affricates of English, respectively. The English affricates are also classified as *sibilants* because they end like sibilant fricatives. Affricates, along with fricatives and oral stops, are referred to as *obstruents* because they involve considerable obstruction in the vocal tract. Table 4 shows the symbols for these sounds.

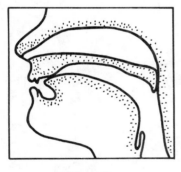

Figure 11a

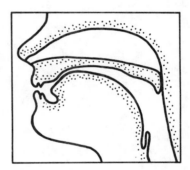

Figure 11b

Table 4.   Affricates of English

Voicing		Place of Articulation
		Palato-Alveolar
	−	tʃ
	+	dʒ

II. Examples: Affricates

The examples that follow illustrate the production of palato-alveolar affricates in different positions within words and in the context of various vowels.

Turn on the tape recorder and follow along.

	Initial	*Final*	*Medial*	*Clusters*
/tʃ/	cheerful	witch	catching	march
	chimney	impeach	ratchet	squelch
	champion	batch	matches	pitched
			peachy	bench
/dʒ/	joyful	bridge	dungeon	orange
	jail	average	midget	barge
	gymnasium	carriage	magic	bulge
			major	dredged

III. SELF-TEST: FRICATIVES AND AFFRICATES

This self-test will assess your ability to recognize and transcribe fricatives and affricates in real and nonsense words. Also, it will give you an indication of what you will need to be able to do by the end of this laboratory session.

In the spaces provided, write the correct symbols for the fricatives and affricates in the real and nonsense words that will now be heard.

Start tape now.

Real words

1. _____   _____   9. _____   _____

2. _____   _____   10. _____   _____

3. _____   _____   11. _____   _____

4. _____   _____   12. _____   _____

5. _____   _____   13. _____   _____

6. _____   _____   14. _____   _____

7. _____   _____   15. _____   _____

8. _____   _____   _____

Nonsense words

16. _____   _____   _____   21. _____   _____   _____

17. _____   _____   _____   22. _____   _____   _____

18. _____   _____   _____   23. _____   _____

19. _____   _____   _____   24. _____   _____

20. _____   _____   _____   25. _____   _____   _____

Check your answers by looking in the back of this workbook.

- If you made 0 to 3 errors, go directly to Exercise G. However, you may wish to do some of the earlier exercises (A–E) for additional practice.
- If you made more than 3 errors, you will need to do all of the following practice exercises.

IV. PRACTICE EXERCISES

The following exercises are graded in difficulty. That is, the last ones will be the hardest. Work at your own pace and write your answers on the forms provided in this workbook.

A. *Yes-No Discriminations*

You will now hear 10 words. For each word indicate whether or not it contains a *fricative*. If it does, check the plus (+) column; if not, check the minus (−) column.

Start tape now.

	+	−		+	−
1.	_____	_____	6.	_____	_____
2.	_____	_____	7.	_____	_____
3.	_____	_____	8.	_____	_____
4.	_____	_____	9.	_____	_____
5.	_____	_____	10.	_____	_____

For each of the following words, indicate whether or not it contains an *affricate*.

	+	−		+	−
11.	_____	_____	14.	_____	_____
12.	_____	_____	15.	_____	_____
13.	_____	_____	16.	_____	_____

For each of the following words, indicate whether or not it contains a *voiced fricative* or *voiced affricate*.

	+	−		+	−
17.	_____	_____	21.	_____	_____
18.	_____	_____	22.	_____	_____
19.	_____	_____	23.	_____	_____
20.	_____	_____	24.	_____	_____

For the following words, indicate whether or not each contains a *sibilant*.

	+	−		+	−
25.	_____	_____	30.	_____	_____
26.	_____	_____	31.	_____	_____
27.	_____	_____	32.	_____	_____
28.	_____	_____	33.	_____	_____
29.	_____	_____	34.	_____	_____

When you are finished with this first exercise, check your answers by looking in the back of this workbook. If you miss more than 2 items, repeat the exercise, paying close attention to the items that gave you difficulty. If you miss 2 or fewer items, go on to Exercise B.

B. Written and Aural Presentation: Specific Positions

Each of the following words contains a fricative or an affricate in the specified position. Write the correct symbol for the fricative or affricate that you hear.

Start tape now.

Initial position

1. _____ civil
2. _____ cherub
3. _____ philodendron
4. _____ thousand
5. _____ voiced
6. _____ then
7. _____ xenon
8. _____ gyroscope
9. _____ hero
10. _____ chambray

Final Position

11. _____ marriage
12. _____ booth
13. _____ sieve
14. _____ mush
15. _____ piece
16. _____ soothe
17. _____ trough
18. _____ garage
19. _____ rose
20. _____ hatch

Medial position

21. _____ too*th*y
22. _____ mar*ch*ing
23. _____ tele*ph*one
24. _____ plea*s*ure
25. _____ an*v*il
26. _____ le*g*ion
27. _____ pa*ss*ion
28. _____ ace*s*
29. _____ limou*s*ine
30. _____ ga*th*er

Clusters

31. _____ *thr*ush
32. _____ *shr*apnel
33. _____ *phr*enetic
34. _____ *str*ong
35. _____ ta*x*
36. _____ loun*ge*
37. _____ len*s*
38. _____ hear*th*
39. _____ ba*thed*
40. _____ por*ch*

41. _____ she*lf*
42. _____ fi*shed*
43. _____ lo*ved*
44. _____ barra*ged*

Now look in the back of this workbook to check your answers. If you made 3 or more errors, you should go back and repeat this lesson. Start with the review of content or with the examples given earlier, and pay particular attention to the sounds that were a problem for you. If you made fewer than 3 errors, go on to Exercise C.

C.   *Aural Only Presentation: Specific Positions*

The lists of words that will now be presented contain fricatives and affricates in specified positions. In each case, write the correct symbol for the fricative or affricate that you hear in the space provided.

Start tape now.

Initial position   *Final position*

1. _____   6. _____   11. _____   16. _____

2. _____   7. _____   12. _____   17. _____

3. _____   8. _____   13. _____   18. _____

4. _____   9. _____   14. _____   19. _____

5. _____   10. _____   15. _____   20. _____

Medial position   *Clusters*

21. _____   26. _____   31. _____   37. _____

22. _____   27. _____   32. _____   38. _____

23. _____   28. _____   33. _____   39. _____

24. _____   29. _____   34. _____   40. _____

25. _____   30. _____   35. _____   41. _____

                                         36. _____   42. _____

Check your answers by looking in the back of this workbook. If you made 3 or more errors, please repeat this exercise. If you made 0 to 2 errors, go on to Exercise D.

D.   Written and Aural Presentation: Combined Positions

The words in the following list contain fricatives and affricates in a variety of word positions and phonetic contexts. In the spaces provided, write the correct symbols for the fricatives or affricates (or both) contained in each word.

Start tape now.

1. _____	machine	13. _____ _____	visionary
2. _____	plaza	14. _____ _____	genies
3. _____	zinc	15. _____ _____	youthful
4. _____	thing	16. _____ _____	smudge
5. _____	either	17. _____ _____	hither
6. _____	enough	18. _____ _____	fetch
7. _____	dash	19. _____ _____	sense
8. _____	kitchen	20. _____ _____	xenolith
9. _____ _____ _____	thrombosis	21. _____ _____	television
10. _____ _____	challenge	22. _____ _____	photography
11. _____ _____	leaves	23. _____ _____	ashes
12. _____ _____	chiffon	24. _____ _____	haze

Go on to the next exercise.

E.   *Aural Only Presentation: Combined Positions—Real Words*

The words that you will now hear contain fricatives and affricates in various positions. In the spaces provided, write the correct symbols for the fricatives and affricates contained in each word.

Start tape now.

1. _____   10. _____   _____
2. _____   11. _____   _____
3. _____   12. _____   _____
4. _____   13. _____   _____
5. _____   14. _____   _____   _____
6. _____   15. _____   _____
7. _____   _____   16. _____   _____
8. _____   _____   17. _____   _____
9. _____   _____   18. _____   _____   _____

Check your answers for these exercises in the back of this workbook. If you made more than 2 errors on either exercise, please repeat that exercise. If you made 0 to 2 errors on both exercises, go directly to Exercise F.

F.   *Aural Only Presentation: Combined Positions—Nonsense Words*

Each nonsense word that will now be heard contains one or more fricatives or affricates, and the positions vary from word to word. In the spaces provided, write the appropriate symbols for the fricatives or affricates (or both) contained in each nonsense word.

Start tape now.

1. _____   8. _____   _____   _____
2. _____   9. _____   _____
3. _____   10. _____   _____   _____
4. _____   11. _____   _____
5. _____   _____   12. _____   _____
6. _____   _____   _____   13. _____   _____
7. _____   _____   _____   14. _____   _____   _____

Check your answers in the back of this book. If you made more than 4 errors, please repeat the exercise. Otherwise, go on to Exercise G.

G. *Sagittal Sections*

Each word that will now be heard contains one fricative. Identify the place of articulation by writing the letter of the appropriate sagittal section (a, b, c, or d) in the space provided.

Start tape now.

1. _____   5. _____

2. _____   6. _____

3. _____   7. _____

4. _____   8. _____

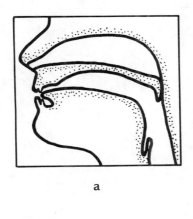

a

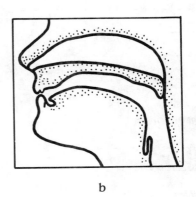

b

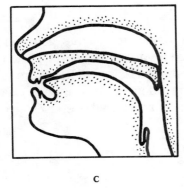

c

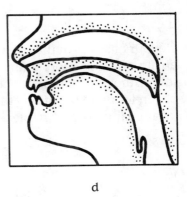

d

Look in the back of this book to see if you made any errors. If you did, then you should repeat the exercise. If you made no errors, good job! Go on to Exercise H.

H.   *Final Exercise: Aural Only Presentation—Combined Positions*

This exercise will help you to identify problems that you may still be having with some fricatives and affricates. In the spaces provided, write the appropriate symbols for the fricatives and affricates that you hear in each real or nonsense word that will now be said.

Start tape now.

Real words

1. _____   9. _____   _____
2. _____   _____   10. _____   _____
3. _____   _____   11. _____   _____
4. _____   _____   _____   12. _____   _____
5. _____   _____   13. _____   _____   _____
6. _____   _____   14. _____   _____   _____
7. _____   _____   15. _____   _____   _____
8. _____   _____

Nonsense words

16. _____   _____   21. _____   _____
17. _____   _____   22. _____   _____
18. _____   _____   23. _____   _____
19. _____   _____   24. _____   _____   _____
20. _____   _____   25. _____   _____   _____

Check your answers in the back of the book. If you made 0 to 3 errors, go on to the test for this lab. If you made more than 3 errors, check to see if your errors correspond to those listed below. If they do, complete the appropriate remedial exercises. (The errors listed below have been found to be among the most common in students' transcriptions.) If your errors do not appear in this chart, please see the instructor for additional exercises.

If you confused:	as in words:	do exercise:
/θ/ and /f/	3,4,6,7,10,13,14,16,18,21,23,25	1
/θ/ and /ð/	3,8,9,10,11,14,16,17,21,22,23	2
/ð/ and /v/	8,10,11,13,15,17,19,20,22,24	3
/dʒ/ and /ʒ/	1,4,5,7,12,15,17,19,20,21,24,25	4
/s/ and /z/	2,4,5,6,8,9,10,14,15,16,25	5

REMEDIAL EXERCISES

These exercises are not on the tape. Each exercise focuses on a particular pair of fricatives or affricates that students frequently find difficult. Say each word over to yourself a few times; then decide which of the two sounds listed occurs in that word and write the appropriate symbol in the space provided. In some cases both sounds occur in one word. In those cases write the symbols in the order in which they occur in the word.

Exercise 1: /ə/ versus /f/

1. _____	berth	6. _____ _____	thief
2. _____	thousand	7. _____	healthy
3. _____	tough	8. _____	shelf
4. _____	fought	9. _____	blithe
5. _____ _____	thrifty	10. _____ _____ _____	fifth

Exercise 2: /ə/ versus /ð/

1. _____	writhe	6. _____	throng
2. _____	wealthy	7. _____	either
3. _____	blither	8. _____	breathing
4. _____	thorough	9. _____	birthday
5. _____	ether	10. _____	heather

Exercise 3: /ð/ versus /v/

1. _____	heave	6. _____	thieves
2. _____	breathe	7. _____	therefore
3. _____	deprive	7. _____	rather
4. _____	grieve	9. _____	gravy
5. _____	neither	10. _____	brother

Exercise 4: /dʒ/ versus /ʒ/

1. _____	mirage	6. _____	pleasure
2. _____	budget	7. _____	visionary
3. _____	gigantic	8. _____	hinge
4. _____	leisure	9. _____	legion
5. _____	carriage	10. _____	television

Exercise 5: /s/ versus /z/

1. _____	faze	6. _____	face
2. _____	loser	7. _____	miser
3. _____	loose	8. _____ _____	business
4. _____ _____	sister	9. _____ _____	seems
5. _____ _____	zeros	10. _____ _____	laces

Check your answers to these exercises in the following section. If you had any trouble with the remedial exercises you completed, go over those words again, focusing on the sounds or symbols that were a problem.

ANSWERS—LABORATORY SESSION 2
REMEDIAL EXERCISES

Exercise 1: /θ/ versus /f/

1.	θ		6.	θ	f
2.	θ		7.	θ	
3.	f		8.	f	
4.	f		9.	θ	
5.	θ	f	10.	f	f	θ

Exercise 2: /θ/ versus /ð/

1.	ð	6.	θ
2.	θ	7.	ð
3.	ð	8.	ð
4.	θ	9.	θ
5.	θ	10.	ð

Exercise 3: /ð/ versus /v/

1.	v	6.	v
2.	ð	7.	ð
3.	v	8.	ð
4.	v	9.	v
5.	ð	10.	ð

Exercise 4: /dʒ/ versus /ʒ/

1.	ʒ	6.	ʒ
2.	dʒ	7.	ʒ
3.	dʒ	8.	dʒ
4.	ʒ	9.	dʒ
5.	dʒ	10.	ʒ

Exercise 5: /s/ versus /z/

1.	z		6.	s	
2.	z		7.	z	
3.	s		8.	z	s
4.	s	s	9.	s	z
5.	z	z	10.	s	z

TEST: FRICATIVES AND AFFRICATES

In the spaces provided, write the correct symbols for the fricatives and affricates in the words that will now be heard. To pass this test and the laboratory session, you will need to make no more than 3 errors on the real words and no more than 3 errors on the nonsense words.

Start tape now.

Real words

1. _____   _____   9. _____   _____   _____
2. _____   _____   10. _____   _____   _____
3. _____   _____   11. _____   _____
4. _____   _____   12. _____   _____
5. _____   _____   13. _____   _____
6. _____   _____   14. _____   _____
7. _____   _____   _____ 15. _____   _____
8. _____   _____

Nonsense words

16. _____   _____   21. _____   _____   _____
17. _____   _____   _____ 22. _____   _____
18. _____   _____   _____ 23. _____   _____   _____
19. _____   _____   _____ 24. _____   _____
20. _____   _____   _____ 25. _____   _____   _____

Laboratory Session 3
Liquids and Glides

OBJECTIVES

In this session you will learn to recognize and transcribe liquids and glides in a variety of positions and contexts in both real and nonsense words. By the end of this session, you will be expected to meet two specific objectives:

- First, when presented with a spoken list of 12 real words containing liquids and glides in various contexts, you will correctly transcribe the liquids and glides with 95% accuracy, without visual cues.
- Second, while listening to 8 nonsense words containing liquids and glides in various contexts, you will correctly transcribe those sounds with 90% accuracy.

AVERAGE TIME (Including Laboratory Review I)

1 hour (range: 30 minutes to 2½ hours)

LIQUIDS AND GLIDES

I.   Review of Content

The sounds covered in this laboratory session are often called *approximants* because, during their production, two articulators are brought close together, but not close enough to create friction. Thus, these sounds are also called *frictionless continuants.*

There is some disagreement regarding which particular sounds are included in this category, what they are called, and how they are described. Two classes of approximants are usually discussed: *liquids* and *glides.* English has just two liquids, /l/ and /r/, as in *lake* and *rake.* Both are voiced, although they may be devoiced in clusters following voiceless consonants.

The two sounds that are nearly always classified as glides are /w/ and /j/, as in *well* and *yell.* They are usually voiced, but, like the liquids, they may be devoiced in certain contexts. In addition to /w/ and /j/, some people classify /h/, as in *help,* as a glottal approximant. As noted earlier, it may also be classified as a fricative. Nothing more will be said here about /h/ because it was included in Laboratory Session 2 with fricatives. In some dialects of English, the initial sound of words such as *which* and *when* is produced not as /w/ but as its voiceless counterpart, /ʍ/, also written as /hw/. Some phoneticians also use /ʍ/ to represent the /w/ glide when it follows a voiceless consonant in words such as *twin* and *sweet.* However, in this laboratory session the /w/ symbol is used. Later on, you will learn about a diacritic that may be used to modify the /w/ symbol in such words to indicate devoicing. Like /h/, /ʍ/ is sometimes classified as a voiceless fricative.

Table 5 contains the symbols for the approximants just described and shows the place of articulation and voicing quality of each one.

Table 5.   Approximants of English

		Place of Articulation			
		Bilabial	Alveolar	Palatal	Velar
Voicing	−	ʍ		r	(ʍ)
	+	w	l	j	(w)

The liquid /l/ is called a *lateral* approximant because air flows out of the oral cavity over the sides of the tongue during its production. The center of the oral cavity, however, is blocked by the tongue. There are actually two distinct /l/ sounds in most dialects of English. When /l/ is produced before a vowel, particularly at the beginning of a word, the tip or blade of the tongue touches the alveolar ridge, as shown in Figure 12a. This type of /l/, as in *lip* and *lamp,* is often called a "light" or "clear" /l/.

When /l/ follows a vowel at the end of a word, as in *bowl,* there is usually an additional raising of the back of the tongue toward the velum. This is shown in Figure 12b. This type of /l/ is called a "dark" /l/. Later on, you will learn to transcribe these two /l/ sounds differently, but for now, use the /l/ symbol for both.

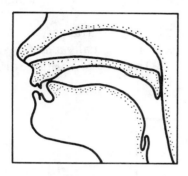

Figure 12a

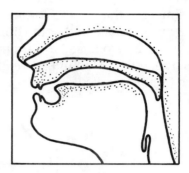

Figure 12b

The other liquid, /r/ (actually /ɹ/ in the IPA, 1978) is quite complicated because it may be produced in a variety of ways, even by the same speaker. During the production of /r/, air flows out of the oral cavity centrally (not laterally, as for /l/). The tongue may be arched toward the soft palate, with the root retracted into the pharynx (MacKay, 1978, p. 124). This is shown in Figure 13a. Alternatively, /r/ may be produced with the blade of the tongue raised toward the palate and the tip of the tongue turned down (Shriberg and Kent, 1982, p. 100). This is shown in Figure 13b. Some speakers produce /r/ with a *retroflex* tongue position. That is, the tip of the tongue is curled up and back toward the alveolar ridge. The tongue body is in the mid-central region of the mouth, and the lips may be rounded (Shriberg and Kent, 1982, p. 99). See Figure 13c.

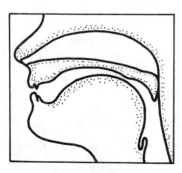

Figure 13a

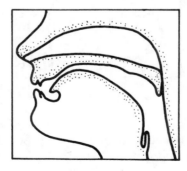

Figure 13b

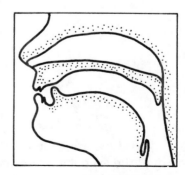

Figure 13c

The liquid /r/ is variously classified as alveolar, alveolo-palatal, or palatal, and it may be called *rhotic, rhotacized,* or *retroflex*. (The vocalic *er* sounds, as in *bird* and *mother* will be covered under central vowels in Laboratory Session 5.)

During the production of the palatal glide /j/, the front of the tongue is raised toward the hard palate, and the tongue tip is behind the lower teeth. See Figure 14. The tongue position for /j/ is very similar to that for the vowel /i/.

The glide /w/ is *bilabial* in that the lips are rounded during its articulation. However, the back of the tongue is also raised toward the soft palate, so it is actually a *labial-velar* consonant. (This is true of the /ʍ/ sound as well.) See Figure 15. The tongue position for /w/ is very similar to that for the vowel /u/.

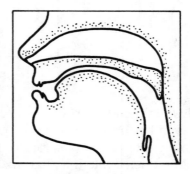

Figure 14

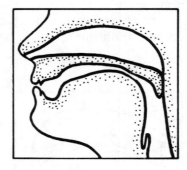

Figure 15

/j/ and /w/ are called *glides* because, during their production, there is a gliding movement of the articulators toward the position of the following vowel. Thus, /j/ and /w/ must be followed by vowels; they do not occur at the ends of words or syllables. (This is also true of /ʍ/ and /h/.) The glides /j/ and /w/ are sometimes called *semi-vowels* because they share certain features with vowels.

II. Examples

The examples that follow illustrate the production of liquids and glides in various positions within words and in the context of various vowels and consonants.

Turn on the tape recorder and follow along.

	Initial	Final	Medial	Clusters
/l/	leap	pile	pillow	blunder
	late	nail	island	sclerosis
	load	ball	align	milk
/r/	reap	tar	merry	bronze
	wring	four	barrette	spring
	rhyme	bear	mortgage	farms
			zero	apart
/j/	yes	—	onion	fuse
	yam		canyon	cube
	use		yoyo	beauty
			dominion	pewter
/w/	weep	—	always	dwell
	water		redwood	dwindle
	once		sandwich	Gwen
			homework	language
/ʌ/	whip	—	bobwhite	
	when		anywhere	
	which		meanwhile	
			overwhelm	

III. Self-Test: Liquids and Glides

This self-test will assess your ability to recognize and transcribe liquids and glides in both real and nonsense words. Also, it will give you an indication of what you will need to be able to do by the end of this session.

In the spaces provided, write the correct symbols for the liquids and glides contained in the real words and nonsense words that will now be heard.

Start tape now.

Real words

1. _____ _____   6. _____ _____
2. _____ _____   7. _____ _____
3. _____ _____   8. _____ _____
4. _____ _____   9. _____ _____
5. _____ _____ _____   10. _____ _____ _____

Nonsense words

11. _____ _____   15. _____ _____ _____
12. _____ _____   16. _____ _____
13. _____ _____ _____   17. _____ _____ _____
14. _____ _____ _____   18. _____ _____

To check your answers, look in the back of your workbook.
- If you made only 1 or 2 errors, go directly to Exercise F. However, you may wish to do some of the earlier exercises for additional practice.
- If you made more than 2 errors, you will need to do all of the exercises in this laboratory session. Go directly to the first practice exercise.

IV. Practice Exercises

The following practice exercises are graded in difficulty. That is, the last ones will be the hardest. Work at your own pace, and write your answers in the spaces provided.

A. *Yes-No Discriminations*

For each word that will now be heard, indicate whether or not it contains a *liquid*. If it does, check the plus (+) column; if it does not, check the minus (–) column.

Start tape now.

	+	–		+	–
1.	_____	_____	5.	_____	_____
2.	_____	_____	6.	_____	_____
3.	_____	_____	7.	_____	_____
4.	_____	_____	8.	_____	_____

Indicate whether or not each word that will now be heard contains a *lateral liquid:*

	+	–		+	–
9.	_____	_____	12.	_____	_____
10.	_____	_____	13.	_____	_____
11.	_____	_____	14.	_____	_____

Indicate whether or not each word that will now be heard contains a *glide:*

	+	–		+	–
15.	_____	_____	19.	_____	_____
16.	_____	_____	20.	_____	_____
17.	_____	_____	21.	_____	_____
18.	_____	_____	22.	_____	_____

Indicate whether or not each word that will now be heard contains a *labial-velar glide:*

	+	–		+	–
23.	_____	_____	26.	_____	_____
24.	_____	_____	27.	_____	_____
25.	_____	_____	28.	_____	_____

When you are finished with this first exercise, check your answers by looking in the back of this workbook. If you miss more than 1 item, repeat the exercise, paying close attention to the items that gave you difficulty. If you miss 0 or 1, go on to the next exercise.

B.   *Aural Only Presentation : Specific Positions*

The words that will now be heard contain liquids and glides in specified positions. In each case, write the correct symbol for the liquid or glide that you hear in the space provided.

Start tape now.

Initial position   *Medial position*

  1. _____   15. _____

  2. _____   16. _____

  3. _____   17. _____

  4. _____   18. _____

  5. _____   19. _____

  6. _____   20. _____

  7. _____   21. _____

  8. _____   22. _____

  9. _____   23. _____

10. _____   24. _____

Final position   *Clusters*

11. _____   25. _____   30. _____

12. _____   26. _____   31. _____

13. _____   27. _____   32. _____

14. _____   28. _____   33. _____

               29. _____   34. _____

Now look in the back of this workbook to check your answers. If you made more than 2 errors, you should go back and repeat this lesson. Start with the review of content or with the examples given earlier, and pay close attention to the sounds that were a problem for you. If you made 2 or fewer errors, continue with Exercise C.

C. *Written and Aural Presentation: Combined Positions*

The words in the following list contain liquids and glides in a variety of positions and contexts. In the spaces provided, write the correct symbols for the liquids and glides that you hear.

Start tape now.

1.	_____		album	11.	_____ _____ _____		wheelbarrow
2.	_____		quince	12.	_____ _____		million
3.	_____		bunion	13.	_____ _____		quickly
4.	_____		woman	14.	_____ _____		nowhere
5.	_____		wren	15.	_____ _____ _____		yardarm
6.	_____ _____		twill	16.	_____ _____		windrow
7.	_____ _____		utilize	17.	_____ _____		redwing
8.	_____ _____		linguist	18.	_____ _____		beautiful
9.	_____ _____		rhinoceros	19.	_____ _____		flaring
10.	_____ _____		memoirs	20.	_____ _____		whistle

Check your answers by looking in the back of this workbook. If you made more than 2 errors, please repeat this exercise. If you made 0 to 2 errors, go on to the next exercise.

D. *Aural Only Presentation: Combined Positions—Real Words*

The words that will now be heard contain liquids and glides in a variety of positions and contexts. In the spaces provided, write the correct symbols for the liquids and glides that you hear.

Start tape now.

1. _____   11. _____   _____
2. _____   12. _____   _____
3. _____   13. _____   _____   _____
4. _____   14. _____   _____
5. _____   15. _____   _____
6. _____   _____   16. _____   _____   _____   _____
7. _____   _____   17. _____   _____
8. _____   _____   18. _____   _____
9. _____   _____   _____   19. _____   _____
10. _____   _____   20. _____   _____

E. *Aural Only Presentation: Combined Positions—Nonsense Words*

The nonsense words that will now be heard contain liquids and glides in various positions and contexts. In the spaces provided, write the correct symbols for the liquids and glides that you hear.

Start tape now.

1. _____   8. _____   _____
2. _____   9. _____   _____   _____
3. _____   10. _____   _____
4. _____   11. _____   _____
5. _____   12. _____   _____
6. _____   _____   13. _____   _____
7. _____   _____   _____   14. _____   _____   _____

Check your answers to these exercises by looking in the back of this workbook. If you made more than 2 errors on either exercise, please do that exercise over. If you made 2 or fewer errors on both exercises, go on to the next exercise.

F. Sagittal Sections

Each word that will now be heard contains one liquid or glide. Identify the place of articulation of that sound by writing the letter of the appropriate sagittal section in the space provided.

Start tape now.

1. _____   6. _____

2. _____   7. _____

3. _____   8. _____

4. _____   9. _____

5. _____   10. _____

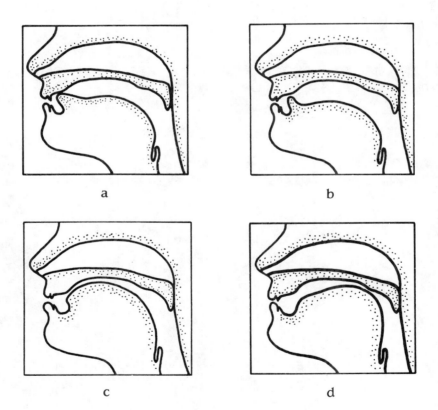

a

b

c

d

Now look in the answer section to see if you made any errors. If you did, you should repeat this exercise. If you made no errors, good job! Go on to the test for Laboratory Session 3.

TEST: LIQUIDS AND GLIDES

In the spaces provided, write the correct symbols for the liquids and glides contained in the real words and nonsense words that will now be heard. To pass this test and laboratory session, you can make no more than 2 errors on the first part of this test and 2 errors on the second part.

Start tape now.

Real words

1. _____ _____ _____   7. _____ _____ _____

2. _____ _____ _____ _____   8. _____ _____

3. _____ _____ _____   9. _____ _____ _____

4. _____ _____   10. _____ _____ _____

5. _____ _____ _____   11. _____ _____

6. _____ _____   12. _____ _____

Nonsense words

13. _____ _____   17. _____ _____

14. _____ _____ _____   18. _____ _____

15. _____ _____ _____   19. _____ _____

16. _____ _____ _____   20. _____ _____ _____

Laboratory Review I
English Consonants

You have now covered all the consonant sounds of standard American English. This review will give you a chance to use all the symbols you have learned.

OBJECTIVES

- First, when presented with a spoken list of 25 real words containing English consonant sounds in a variety of word positions, you will correctly transcribe all the consonants with 95% accuracy (without visual cues).
- Second, while listening to 15 nonsense words containing all English consonants in a variety of word positions, you will correctly transcribe the consonant sounds with 95% accuracy.

PRACTICE EXERCISE: ENGLISH CONSONANTS

In the spaces provided, write the correct symbols for the consonants contained in the real and nonsense words that will now be heard.

Start tape now.

Real words

1. ___ ___ ___ ___ ___ ___						11. ___ ___ ___ ___ ___				
2. ___ ___ ___ ___						12. ___ ___ ___		
3. ___ ___ ___ ___ ___						13. ___ ___ ___ ___			
4. ___ ___ ___ ___ ___						14. ___ ___ ___ ___ ___				
5. ___ ___ ___ ___ ___						15. ___ ___ ___ ___ ___				
6. ___ ___ ___ ___						16. ___ ___ ___ ___			
7. ___ ___ ___ ___						17. ___ ___ ___ ___			
8. ___ ___ ___ ___						18. ___ ___ ___ ___ ___				
9. ___ ___ ___ ___ ___						19. ___ ___ ___ ___			
10. ___ ___ ___ ___						20. ___ ___ ___ ___ ___				

Nonsense words

21. ___ ___ ___						26. ___ ___ ___ ___ ___				
22. ___ ___ ___						27. ___ ___ ___ ___			
23. ___ ___ ___ ___ ___						28. ___ ___ ___ ___ ___ ___					
24. ___ ___ ___ ___						29. ___ ___ ___ ___ ___				
25. ___ ___ ___ ___						30. ___ ___ ___ ___			

Check your answers in the back of this book. If you made more than 4 errors on the real words or 2 errors on the nonsense words, please repeat the exercise. Otherwise, go on to the test for Laboratory Review I.

TEST: ENGLISH CONSONANTS

Start tape now.

Real words

1. _____ _____ _____ _____

2. _____ _____ _____ _____ _____

3. _____ _____ _____

4. _____ _____ _____

5. _____ _____ _____

6. _____ _____ _____

7. _____ _____ _____

8. _____ _____ _____ _____

9. _____ _____ _____ _____

10. _____ _____ _____ _____ _____

11. _____ _____ _____

12. _____ _____ _____ _____

13. _____ _____

14. _____ _____ _____ _____

15. _____ _____ _____

16. _____ _____ _____ _____

17. _____ _____ _____

18. _____ _____ _____

19. _____ _____ _____ _____

20. _____ _____ _____ _____

21. _____ _____ _____ _____ _____ _____ _____

22. _____ _____ _____ _____

23. _____ _____ _____ _____ _____ _____

24. _____ _____ _____

25. _____ _____ _____

Nonsense words

26. _____ _____ _____ _____

27. _____ _____ _____

28. _____ _____ _____ _____

29. _____ _____ _____ _____ _____ _____

30. _____ _____ _____ _____

31. _____ _____ _____ _____

32. _____ _____ _____ _____

33. _____ _____ _____ _____ _____

34. _____ _____ _____ _____ _____

35. _____ _____ _____

36. _____ _____ _____

37. _____ _____ _____ _____

38. _____ _____ _____ _____

39. _____ _____ _____ _____

40. _____ _____ _____ _____

In the spaces provided, write the correct symbols for the consonants contained in the real and nonsense words that will now be heard. To pass this test, you must make no more than 5 errors on the real words and 3 errors on the nonsense words. Turn this test in at the next class, along with the test for Laboratory Session 3.

Laboratory Session 4
Front and Back Vowels

OBJECTIVES

In this session you will learn to recognize and transcribe front and back vowel sounds in a variety of positions and contexts in both real and nonsense words. By the end of this session you will be expected to meet two specific objectives:

- First, when presented with a list of 12 real words containing front and back vowels in various contexts, you will correctly transcribe those vowels with 95% accuracy, without visual cues.
- Second, while listening to 8 nonsense words containing a variety of front and back vowel sounds, you will correctly transcribe those vowels with 90% accuracy.

AVERAGE TIME

$1^1/_3$ hours (range: 35 minutes to $2^1/_4$ hours)

FRONT AND BACK VOWELS

I. Review of Content

Vowels sounds differ from consonants in that they are produced with a more open vocal tract. They are also naturally voiced; thus they do not occur in voiceless or voiced cognate pairs. In addition, vowels are categorized differently. Rather than being described in terms of place, manner, and voicing, as consonants are, they are classified according to tongue position (front, central, or back), tongue height (high, mid, or low), and lip shape (rounded or spread). They may also be described according to jaw position (closed, mid, or open) and tenseness (tense or lax).

Vowels often differ considerably from one dialect of English to another. Therefore, it is not feasible to include in these laboratory sessions all the vowel sounds that may occur in English. Instead, 14 vowel sounds that are usually said to occur in General American English or other common varieties of English are covered in Laboratory Sessions 4 and 5. All of these vowels are presented in the following chart. Tongue height and position and lip rounding, as well as jaw height, are shown for each vowel. In Laboratory Session 4 we focus only on the front and back vowels. The central vowels are covered in Laboratory Session 5.

ENGLISH VOWELS

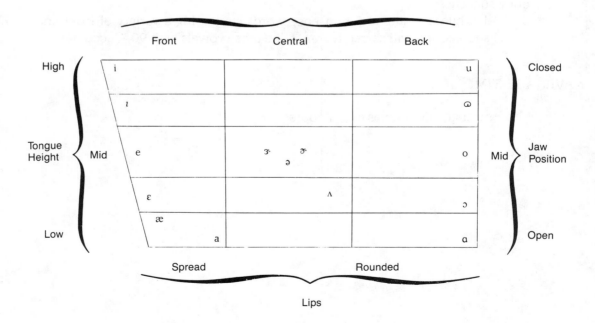

A. Front Vowels

The front vowels that are usually discussed, from high to low, are /i/, /ɪ/, /e/, /ɛ/, /æ/. These vowels are produced without lip rounding. During the production of the /i/ vowel, as in *beet,* the front of the tongue is raised toward the hard palate, the tongue tip is behind the lower front teeth, and the lips are held slightly apart. /i/ is produced with the tongue as high and as far forward in the mouth as possible for the production of a vowel. /i/ is called a *tense* vowel because of the muscular tension in the tongue during its production.

The high-mid vowel /ɪ/ or /ɪ/, as in *bit,* is also produced by raising the front of the tongue toward the palate. However, the tongue is not raised as much and is not quite as far forward as for /i/, and there is less muscular tension. Thus, /ɪ/ is often considered to be the *lax* counterpart of /i/. See Figures 16 (/i/) and 17 (/ɪ/).

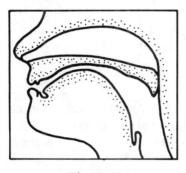

Figure 16

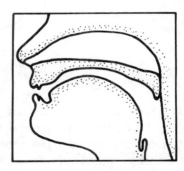

Figure 17

The front mid vowel /e/, as in *bait,* is produced with still less constriction in the palatal region. That is, the tongue is lower than for /ɪ/. /e/ is a tense vowel. The "pure" (non-diphthongized) /e/ sound occurs mainly in unstressed syllables and in stressed syllables when the following sound is a voiceless consonant, especially a stop. (The diphthong /eɪ/ will be covered in Laboratory Session 5.)

The low-mid vowel /ɛ/ ("epsilon"), as in *bet,* is produced with the jaw somewhat more open than for /e/; the front of the tongue is raised just slightly toward the palate. There is little muscular tension in the tongue during its production. In fact, /ɛ/ is generally considered to be the lax counterpart of /e/. See Figures 18 (/e/) and 19 (/ɛ/).

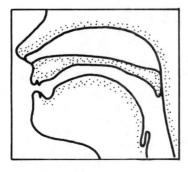

Figure 18

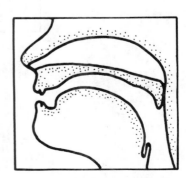

Figure 19

The low front vowel /æ/ ("ash"), as in *bat,* is produced with the jaw more open than for /ɛ/. The lips may be retracted. There is some disagreement as to whether /æ/ should be considered a tense or lax vowel. There is relatively little muscular tension during its production, but it "lasts" a relatively long time, as do tense vowels. The production of /æ/ is represented in Figure 20.

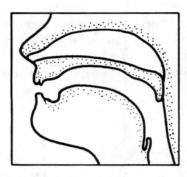

Figure 20

For many speakers of English, /æ/ is the lowest front vowel. However, in certain other languages (e.g., French) and in some dialects of English there is another vowel, transcribed as /a/, that is produced with the jaw more open and with the tongue back somewhat further than for /æ/. This vowel occurs in some Eastern dialects of American English for *ar,* as in *park* and *car.* In these dialects /a/ may also occur in place of /æ/ in words such as *path* and *laughter.* Because of its marginal status in American English, the vowel /a/ will not be included in the exercises in this laboratory session. See Figure 21.

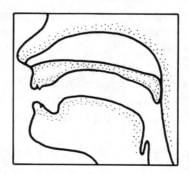

Figure 21

B. *Back Vowels*

The back vowels that are generally said to occur in American English are, from high to low, /u/, /ʊ/, /o/, /ɔ/, /ɑ/. Unlike the front vowels of English, the back vowels—with the exception of /ɑ/—are produced with lip rounding.

The high back vowel /u/, as in *boot,* is produced with the back of the tongue raised toward the soft palate, almost touching it. The tip of the tongue is behind the lower front teeth. The jaw is nearly closed. The lips are rounded and may be protruded. The tongue root may also be "advanced," resulting in a widened pharynx. /u/ is a tense vowel. See Figure 22.

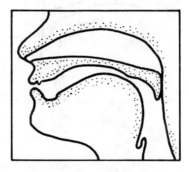

Figure 22

During the production of the high-mid back vowel /ʊ/ (or /ʊ/), as in *book*, the back of the tongue is also raised toward the velum, but it is not as high or as tense as for /u/. The jaw is almost closed, but the lips are not as rounded as they are in the production of /u/. See Figure 23.

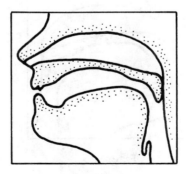

Figure 23

The back mid vowel /o/, as in *boat,* is produced with the tongue lower than for /ʊ/ but still raised toward the soft palate. The lips are rounded and may be protruded. /o/ is a tense vowel. The "pure" (non-diphthongized) /o/ sound occurs in English mainly in unstressed syllables and in stressed syllables when the following sound is a voiceless consonant, especially a stop. (The /oʊ/ diphthong will be covered in Laboratory Session 5.) See Figure 24.

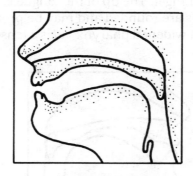

Figure 24

The low-mid back vowel /ɔ/ ("open o"), as in *law,* is produced with the back of the tongue raised slightly less than for /o/ and with the jaw more open. The lips are rounded, but less so than for /u/ and /o/. Some phoneticians consider /ɔ/ to be a tense vowel, but others do not. There is a great deal of dialectal variation regarding the occurrence of /ɔ/, and in some dialects /ɑ/ is nearly always used instead of /ɔ/. The production of /ɔ/ is represented in Figure 25.

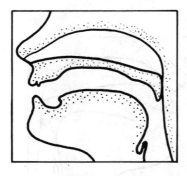

Figure 25

The vowel /ɑ/, as in *ah,* is produced with the tongue in the low back position. The root of the tongue is retracted into the pharynx, and the jaw is open more than for any other vowel of American English. The lips are not rounded. /ɑ/ is generally considered to be a tense vowel. Dialects differ a great deal regarding their use of /ɑ/. In some dialects /ɑ/ is used in place of /ɔ/, as noted earlier. Figure 26 is a schematic representation of the production of /ɑ/.

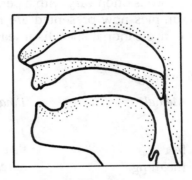

Figure 26

It should be pointed out that not all vowels can occur in all positions within words. For example, /ɛ/, /æ/, /ɑ/, and the central vowel /ʌ/ (as in *cut*), do not occur in final position, and /ɪ/ occurs in that position only in words such as *pretty* or *city* in some dialects. /ɑ/ occurs in final position only in a few words such as *pa* and *ma.* /ɔ/ does not occur in word-initial position, and /u/ occurs only rarely in that position. Also note that vowels are affected by neighboring sounds. For example, the /æ/ vowel sounds quite different in *can, bat,* and *pal.* Later you will learn to capture some of these differences in your transcriptions.

II. Examples

The examples that will now be presented illustrate the production of the vowels just discussed. While listening to these examples, please keep in mind that your production of the vowels in some of these words may differ from that of the speaker on the tape. Because vowels often differ considerably from dialect to dialect, it is difficult to find "key words" on which speakers agree. In addition, vowels often vary with a person's rate of speech and carefulness of pronunciation. The examples now presented are read in a relatively slow and careful style. If they occurred in conversational speech, at least some of the vowels would change.

Turn on the tape recorder and follow along.

	Initial	*Medial*	*Final*
Front Vowels			
/i/	either	feet	flea
	eat	meaning	agree
		repeat	handy
			cookie*
/ɪ/	ill	bin	—
	inner	timber	
		mixing	
/e/	ape	baked	foray
	eighteen	operation	holiday
		locate	
/ɛ/	anyone	melt	—
	Emily	length	
		pretend	
/æ/	attic	hand	—
	anxious	banana	
		matter	

*Phoneticians do not agree regarding how to transcribe the final vowel in words such as *handy* and *cookie*. Many phoneticians prefer to use /ɪ/. However, we will use /i/ here.

Back Vowels

/u/	*oo*zy	flute	cr*ew*
		recr*ui*t	imb*ue*
		r*ou*lette	
/ʊ/	—	p*u*ll	—
		sh*ou*ld	
		f*u*lfill	
/o/	*o*pen	h*o*peful	tomorr*ow*
	*o*cean	m*o*tor	s*o*lo
		f*o*lks	
/ɔ/	*aw*ful	br*ou*ght	l*aw*
	*aw*l	f*au*lty	dr*aw*
		wr*o*ng	
/ɑ/	*a*lms	al*a*rm	h*a*
	*a*rtist	h*ea*rt	p*a*
		gu*a*rdian	

III. Self-Test: Front and Back Vowels

This self-test will assess your ability to recognize and transcribe front and back vowels in both real and nonsense words. Also, it will give you an indication of what you should be able to do by the end of this session.

In the spaces provided, write the correct symbols for the front and back vowels contained in the real words and nonsense words that will now be read.

Start tape now.

Real words

1. _____ _____   7. _____ _____ _____
2. _____ _____   8. _____ _____ _____
3. _____ _____   9. _____ _____ _____
4. _____ _____   10. _____ _____ _____ _____
5. _____ _____ _____   11. _____ _____ _____ _____
6. _____ _____ _____   12. _____ _____ _____ _____

Nonsense words

13. _____ _____   17. _____ _____ _____
14. _____ _____   18. _____ _____ _____
15. _____ _____   19. _____ _____ _____ _____
16. _____ _____   20. _____ _____ _____ _____

Check your answers by looking in the back of the book.
- If you made only 3 (or fewer) errors, go directly to Exercise E. However, you may wish to do some of the earlier exercises for additional practice with these vowel sounds.
- If you made 4 or more errors, you will need to do all of the exercises in this laboratory session. Go directly to the first practice exercise.

IV. Practice Exercises

The following exercises are graded in difficulty. That is, the last ones are the hardest. Work at your own pace, and write your answers in the appropriate spaces.

A. *Yes-No Discriminations*

For each word that will now be heard, indicate whether or not it contains a *front vowel*.

Start tape now.

	+	−		+	−
1.	____	____	6.	____	____
2.	____	____	7.	____	____
3.	____	____	8.	____	____
4.	____	____	9.	____	____
5.	____	____	10.	____	____

Indicate whether or not each word that will now be heard contains a *back vowel*.

	+	−		+	−
11.	____	____	16.	____	____
12.	____	____	17.	____	____
13.	____	____	18.	____	____
14.	____	____	19.	____	____
15.	____	____	20.	____	____

Check your answers by looking in the back of this workbook. If you missed more than 1 item, repeat this exercise, paying close attention to the items that gave you difficulty. If you didn't miss any, or missed only 1, go on to the next exercise.

B.   Written and Aural Presentation: Combined Positions—Subclasses of Vowels

The words that will now be heard contain subclasses of vowels (front or back) in a variety of positions and contexts. In each case, write the correct symbols for the vowels that you hear in the spaces provided.

Start tape now.

Front vowels

1.	_____	bake	8.	_____		tricks
2.	_____	fish	9.	_____		steep
3.	_____	grief	10.	_____		scent
4.	_____	tax	11.	_____	_____	banish
5.	_____	cape	12.	_____	_____	relate
6.	_____	tense	13.	_____	_____	vexing
7.	_____	flash	14.	_____	_____	event

Back vowels

15.	_____	soak	22.	_____		vault
16.	_____	tube	23.	_____		boast
17.	_____	lawn	24.	_____		shook
18.	_____	full	25.	_____	_____	solo
19.	_____	balm	26.	_____	_____	borrow
20.	_____	cute	27.	_____	_____	boat hook
21.	_____	farm	28.	_____	_____	follow

Now look in the back of this workbook to check your answers. If you made more than 2 errors, please repeat this exercise. Otherwise, go on to Exercise C.

C.   Aural Only Presentation: Specific Positions

The lists of words that will now be heard contain front and back vowels in specific positions. In each case, write the correct symbol for the vowel sound that you hear in the space provided.

Start tape now.

Initial Position

1. _____   6. _____
2. _____   7. _____
3. _____   8. _____
4. _____   9. _____
5. _____   10. _____

Medial position

11. _____   16. _____
12. _____   17. _____
13. _____   18. _____
14. _____   19. _____
15. _____   20. _____

Final position

21. _____   24. _____
22. _____   25. _____
23. _____   26. _____

Now look in the back of this workbook to check your answers. If you made more than 2 errors, you should go back and repeat this lesson, beginning with the review of content or the examples and focusing on the sounds that were a problem for you. If you made 2 or fewer errors, go on to Exercise D.

D.   Written and Aural Presentation: Combined Positions

The words in the following list contain front and back vowel sounds in a variety of contexts and positions. In the spaces provided, write the correct symbols for the vowels that you hear.

Start tape now.

1.	_____	proof	11.	_____	_____	input
2.	_____	goat	12.	_____	_____	oolong
3.	_____	leaf	13.	_____	_____	message
4.	_____	crawl	14.	_____	_____	losing
5.	_____	sift	15.	_____	_____	barroom
6.	_____	dressed	16.	_____	_____	kidney
7.	_____	haste	17.	_____	_____	bootcamp
8.	_____	could	18.	_____	_____	_____	symmetric
9.	_____	fast	19.	_____	_____	_____	narrowly
10.	_____	barn	20.	_____	_____	_____	_____	initiate

Check your answers in the back of this workbook. If you missed more than 2 items, please repeat the exercise. Otherwise go on to Exercise E.

E.   Aural Only Presentation: Combined Positions

The words that will now be heard contain front and back vowels in a variety of positions and contexts. In the spaces provided, write the correct symbols for the vowels that you hear.

Start tape now.

1.	_____	11.	_____	_____	
2.	_____	12.	_____	_____	
3.	_____	13.	_____	_____	
4.	_____	14.	_____	_____	
5.	_____	15.	_____	_____	
6.	_____	16.	_____	_____	
7.	_____	17.	_____	_____	_____
8.	_____	18.	_____	_____	_____
9.	_____	19.	_____	_____	_____
10.	_____	20.	_____	_____	_____	_____

Now check your answers to this exercise in the back of this book. If you made more than 2 errors, please do the exercise over. If you made 0 to 2 errors, go on to the next exercise.

F.   Aural Only Presentation: Combined Positions—Nonsense Words

The nonsense words that will now be heard contain front and back vowels in a variety of positions and contexts. In the spaces provided, write the correct symbols for the vowels that you hear.

Start tape now.

1. _____   11. _____   _____
2. _____   12. _____   _____
3. _____   13. _____   _____
4. _____   14. _____   _____
5. _____   15. _____   _____
6. _____   16. _____   _____   _____
7. _____   17. _____   _____   _____
8. _____   18. _____   _____   _____
9. _____   19. _____   _____   _____
10. _____   20. _____   _____   _____   _____

Now check your answers to this exercise in the back of this book. If you made more than 3 errors, please do the exercise over. If you made 0 to 3 errors, congratulations! You are now ready to take the test for this laboratory session.

TEST: FRONT AND BACK VOWELS

In the spaces provided, write the correct symbols for the front and back vowels contained in both the real words and the nonsense words that will now be heard. To pass this laboratory session, you can make only 2 errors on the first part (real words) and only 2 errors on the second part (nonsense words).

Start tape now.

Real words

1. _____ _____   7. _____ _____ _____

2. _____ _____   8. _____ _____ _____

3. _____ _____   9. _____ _____ _____

4. _____ _____   10. _____ _____ _____ _____

5. _____ _____ _____   11. _____ _____ _____ _____

6. _____ _____ _____   12. _____ _____ _____ _____

Nonsense words

13. _____ _____   17. _____ _____ _____

14. _____ _____   18. _____ _____ _____

15. _____ _____   19. _____ _____ _____ _____

16. _____ _____   20. _____ _____ _____ _____

Laboratory Session 5
Central Vowels and Diphthongs

OBJECTIVES

In this laboratory session you will learn to recognize and transcribe central vowels and diphthongs in a variety of positions and contexts in both real and nonsense words. By the end of this session you will be expected to meet two specific objectives:

- First, when presented with a list of 15 real words containing central vowels and diphthongs in various contexts, you will correctly transcribe those vowels and diphthongs with 95% accuracy, without visual cues.
- Second, while listening to 10 nonsense words containing a variety of central vowels and diphthongs, you will correctly transcribe those vowels and diphthongs with 90% accuracy.

AVERAGE TIME (Including Laboratory Review II)

2 hours (range: 45 minutes to 3 hours)

NOTE: This laboratory session consists of two parts: Part A (central vowels) and Part B (diphthongs). Because this is a long session, you may want to do the two parts separately. However, the test at the end covers both parts of the laboratory session, so you will want to review Part A before taking the test.

PART A
CENTRAL VOWELS

I. Review of Content

As noted in Laboratory Session 4, vowel sounds differ from consonants in that they are produced with a more open vocal tract and are also naturally voiced. Laboratory Session 4 focused on vowels produced in the front of the mouth and those produced in the back of the mouth. In this laboratory session we focus on central vowels (see diagram) and on diphthongs (described later).

ENGLISH VOWELS

Tongue Position

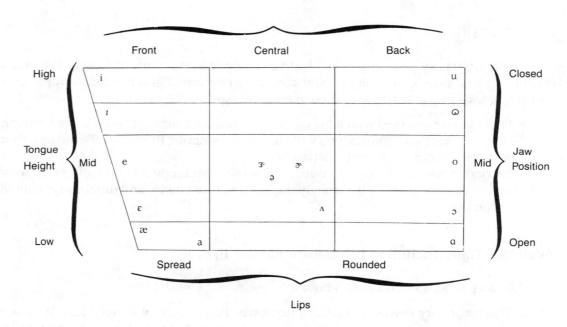

Lips

The /ʌ/ vowel, as in *but,* is a low-mid, unrounded vowel. It is also classified as lax be-cause the tongue muscles are not tense during its production. Although /ʌ/ is included here with the central vowels (as is customary), the tongue is actually somewhat lower and further back than for the central vowels. Thus, it is sometimes considered to be a back vowel. The tongue position for the production of /ʌ/ is shown in Figure 27.

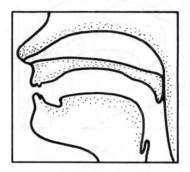

Figure 27

The schwa vowel (/ə/), as in the first sound of *about,* is often considered to be the un-stressed counterpart of /ʌ/. For instance, in the word *above* [əˈbʌv], both unstressed schwa and stressed /ʌ/ occur.* /ə/ is produced with the tongue in the mid-central region of the mouth. The tongue muscles are more relaxed than for /ʌ/, and /ə/ lasts a shorter time. In fact, the tongue may simply pass through the mid-central region in moving from the position for the preceding sound to that of the following sound (Shriberg and Kent, 1982, p. 51). In casual speech, many unstressed vowels are produced as schwa. See Figure 28.

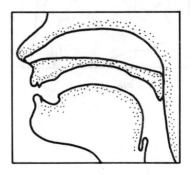

Figure 28

---

*A short raised vertical line indicates that the syllable immediately following has main stress (see Laboratory Session 7).

Another mid-central vowel is the *r*-colored /ɚ/ sound, sometimes referred to as "schwar." Schwar is a lax vowel, and it occurs only in unstressed position, as in the last sound of *butter*. It may be produced with lip rounding. See Figure 29.

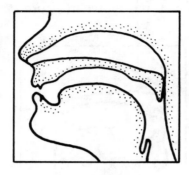

Figure 29

The stressed counterpart of schwar is the *r*-colored (or retroflex or rhotacized) /ɝ/ vowel, as in *bird*. It is produced with a mid-central tongue position and often with some lip rounding. /ɝ/ lasts longer than /ɚ/ and involves more muscular tension. See Figure 30.

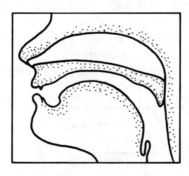

Figure 30

II. Examples

The examples that will now be presented illustrate the production of the vowels just discussed. While listening to these examples, please keep in mind that your production of the vowels in some of these words may differ from that of the speaker on the tape.

Now turn on the tape recorder and follow along.

	Initial	*Medial*	*Final*
/ʌ/	other ultimate	mother enough above	—
/ə/	above enough	moment demon balloon	sofa zebra
/ɚ/	urbane ergometer	pertain curtail injured	mother harbor
/ɝ/	urbanite earnest	herd curtain thirty	infer defer

III.   Self-Test: Central Vowels

This self-test will assess your ability to recognize and transcribe central vowels in both real and nonsense words. Also, it will give you an indication of what you will need to be able to do by the end of this laboratory session.

In the spaces provided, write the correct symbols for the central vowels contained in the real words and nonsense words that will now be heard.

Start tape now.

Real words

1. _____ _____   6. _____ _____
2. _____ _____   7. _____ _____
3. _____ _____   8. _____ _____ _____
4. _____ _____   9. _____ _____ _____
5. _____ _____   10. _____ _____ _____

Nonsense words

11. _____ _____   15. _____ _____ _____
12. _____ _____   16. _____ _____ _____
13. _____ _____ _____   17. _____ _____ _____
14. _____ _____ _____   18. _____ _____ _____ _____

Check your answers in the back of the book.
- If you made only 3 (or fewer) errors, go directly to Exercise E. However, you may wish to do some of the earlier exercises for additional practice with these sounds.
- If you made more than 3 errors, you will need to do all of the exercises in this part of Laboratory Session 5. Go directly to the first practice exercise.

IV.   Practice Exercises

The following exercises are graded in difficulty. That is, the last ones are the hardest. Work at your own pace and write your answers in the appropriate spaces.

A.   *Yes-No Discriminations*

Indicate whether or not each word that will now be heard contains a *central vowel.*

Start tape now.

	+	−		+	−
1.	_____	_____	5.	_____	_____
2.	_____	_____	6.	_____	_____
3.	_____	_____	7.	_____	_____
4.	_____	_____	8.	_____	_____

Indicate whether or not each word that will now be heard contains /ʌ/.

	+	−		+	−
9.	_____	_____	12.	_____	_____
10.	_____	_____	13.	_____	_____
11.	_____	_____	14.	_____	_____

Indicate whether or not each word that will now be heard contains /ɝ/.

	+	−		+	−
15.	_____	_____	18.	_____	_____
16.	_____	_____	19.	_____	_____
17.	_____	_____	20.	_____	_____

Indicate whether or not each word that will now be heard contains /ə/.

	+	−		+	−
21.	_____	_____	23.	_____	_____
22.	_____	_____	24.	_____	_____

Indicate whether or not each word that will now be heard contains /ɚ/.

	+	−		+	−
25.	_____	_____	27.	_____	_____
26.	_____	_____	28.	_____	_____

Check your answers in the back of this workbook. If you missed any items, repeat this exercise, paying close attention to the items that gave you difficulty. If you didn't miss any, go on to the next exercise.

B. *Aural Only Presentation: Specific Positions*

The lists of words that will be heard contain central vowels in specific positions. In each case, write the correct symbol for the vowel sound that you hear in the space provided.

Start tape now.

Initial position

1. _____   4. _____

2. _____   5. _____

3. _____   6. _____

Medial position

7. _____   10. _____

8. _____   11. _____

9. _____   12. _____

Final position

13. _____   16. _____

14. _____   17. _____

15. _____   18. _____

Now look in the back of this workbook to check your answers. If you made more than 1 error, you should go back and repeat this lesson, beginning with the review of content or the examples and focusing on the sounds that were a problem for you. If you made 0 or 1 error, go on to Exercise C.

C. *Written and Aural Presentation: Combined Positions*

The words that will now be heard contain central vowel sounds in a variety of contexts and positions. In the spaces provided, write the correct symbols for the central vowels that you hear.

Start tape now.

1. _____   mutt   6. _____ _____   surplus

2. _____   dirt   7. _____ _____   undone

3. _____ _____   brother   8. _____ _____ _____   murderous

4. _____ _____   above   9. _____ _____ _____   thunderstruck

5. _____ _____   murmur   10. _____ _____ _____   uncover

Go on to the next exercise.

D. *Aural Only Presentation: Combined Positions*

The words you will now hear contain central vowels in a variety of positions and contexts. In the spaces provided, write the correct symbols for the central vowels that you hear.

Start tape now.

1. _____   6. _____   _____
2. _____   7. _____   _____
3. _____   _____   8. _____   _____   _____
4. _____   _____   9. _____   _____   _____
5. _____   _____   10. _____   _____   _____   _____

Now check your answers to these exercises in the back of this workbook. If you made more than 1 error on either exercise, please do that exercise over. If you made 0 or 1 error, go on to the next exercise.

E. *Aural Only Presentation: Combined Positions—Nonsense Words*

The words that will now be heard contain central vowels in a variety of positions and contexts. In the spaces provided, write the correct symbols for the central vowels that you hear.

Start tape now.

1. _____   6. _____   _____   _____
2. _____   7. _____   _____   _____
3. _____   _____   8. _____   _____   _____
4. _____   _____   9. _____   _____   _____
5. _____   _____   10. _____   _____   _____   _____

Check your answers in the back of this workbook. If you made more than 2 errors, please repeat this exercise. If you made only 0 to 2 errors, you are ready to do the final exercise for Part A of this laboratory session.

F.   Final Exercise: Central Vowels

In the spaces provided, write the correct symbols for the central vowels contained in the real words and nonsense words that will now be heard.

Start tape now.

Real words

1.   _____   8.   _____   _____

2.   _____   9.   _____   _____

3.   _____   10. _____   _____

4.   _____   11. _____   _____

5.   _____   _____   12. _____   _____   _____

6.   _____   _____   13. _____   _____   _____

7.   _____   _____   14. _____   _____   _____

Nonsense words

15. _____   _____   18. _____   _____   _____

16. _____   _____   19. _____   _____   _____

17. _____   _____   _____   20. _____   _____   _____   _____

Check your answers in the back of this workbook. If you made more than 3 errors, go back to the review of content and the examples given for this part of Laboratory Session 5. Then redo this final exercise. If you made 3 or fewer errors, good job! You are ready to go on to the second part of this laboratory session.

PART B
DIPHTHONGS

I. Review of Content

A *diphthong* can be defined as two vowel sounds together in the same syllable, as a two-part vowel, or as a vowel that changes in quality. That is, the articulators begin in the position for one vowel, sometimes called the *onglide,* and end in the position for another vowel, sometimes called the *offglide.* In other words, the point of articulation of the vowel changes during its production. Thus, diphthongs are "complex" vowels. Like monophthongs (or pure vowels), diphthongs are produced with a relatively unobstructed vocal tract and are naturally voiced.

Different dialects of English may differ considerably in the diphthongs that they contain; in some dialects many vowels are diphthongized, for example, [peət] for *Pat.* However, General American English is usually said to have five diphthong sounds, shown in the chart below. It should be noted that there are several different systems for transcribing diphthongs, and ligatures (or connecting lines) are sometimes used to show that the two vowels joined by the line are part of one syllable, for example, [eə]. In this chart, the arrows represent the direction of tongue movement during the production of each diphthong.

ENGLISH DIPHTHONGS

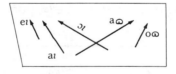

Two of the diphthongs used in English are the diphthongized or complex counterparts of the mid front vowel /e/ and the mid back vowel /o/. As discussed in Laboratory Session 4, the "pure" mid vowels /e/ and /o/ are usually said to occur only in specific contexts in many dialects of English. The corresponding diphthongs, /eɪ/ (or /eɪ/) and /oʊ/ (or /oʊ/), typically occur in stressed "open" syllables (i.e., syllables without final consonants), such as *bay* and *low.* They also often occur in syllables preceding liquids, nasals, and voiced obstruents (e.g., *bale* and *bone*). In some contexts, the extent (if any) to which these vowels are diphthongized depends on the speaker's rate and style of speaking. In such cases, these sounds should simply be transcribed as they are perceived, either as monophthongs ([e] ,[o]) or as diphthongs ([eɪ], [oʊ]). It is important to point out that the difference between [e] and [eɪ] and between [o] and [oʊ], although perceptible, is not a "significant" difference in English. That is, the difference is never used to distinguish two otherwise identical words. To illustrate, [bel] and [beɪl] are not two different words in English, but simply variant pronunciations of the word *bale* (or *bail*).

During the production of /eɪ/, as in *say* or *fail,* the tongue begins in the position for an /e/ vowel and rises to the position for a high front vowel. This is shown schematically in Figure 31. The solid line represents the /e/ position or onglide, and the broken line represents the position for the offglide /ɪ/.

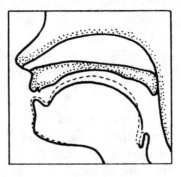

Figure 31

During the production of /oʊ/, as in *sew* or *bowl,* the tongue begins in the position for /o/ and glides upward to end in the position for a high back vowel (/ʊ/, or a vowel between /u/ and /ʊ/). Both parts of this diphthong are produced with lip rounding. The production of /oʊ/ is represented schematically in Figure 32. The solid line represents the /o/ or onglide portion of the diphthong, and the broken line represents the /ʊ/ portion or offglide.

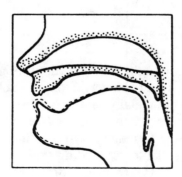

Figure 32

The other three diphthongs of English are /aɪ/, as in *buy,* /aʊ/ as in *brow,* and /ɔɪ/, as in *boy.* Unlike /eɪ/ and /oʊ/, these diphthongs have no "pure" counterparts. They are produced as diphthongs regardless of the surrounding sounds or the stress pattern of the word or the rate of speech. In some dialects, these diphthongs may be replaced by pure vowels, as in [ma] for *my,* but this does not happen in General American English. When these diphthongs are not stressed or when the rate of speech is rapid, they may sound more centralized and shorter, but, by convention, they are still transcribed as /aɪ/, /aʊ/, and /ɔɪ/. These diphthongs are also affected by the surrounding sounds, particularly the following consonant. Although the symbols just listed are generally used, regardless of phonetic context, they may be modified by diacritics to show variations in pronunciation.

The diphthong /aɪ/ (or /aɪ/), as in *buy, invite,* or *myopic,* begins with the tongue in a low position (as for /a/ or /ɑ/). The tongue then moves up and forward to the position for a high front vowel (/ɪ/ or a vowel between /ɪ/ and /i/). The jaw is also raised. This diphthong is produced without lip rounding. The production of /aɪ/ is represented schematically in Figure 33.

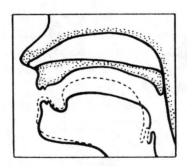

Figure 33

The diphthong /aɷ/ (or /aʊ/), as in *cow, about,* or *outing,* begins with the tongue in a low position. It then moves upward toward the position for a high back vowel. The jaw is also raised, and the lips become rounded. See Figure 34.

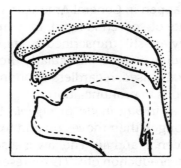

Figure 34

Finally, the /ɔɪ/ (or ɔɪ/) diphthong, as in *boy, noisy,* and *boisterous,* begins with the tongue, lips, and jaw in the position for /ɔ/ (a low-mid, rounded back vowel). The tongue then moves upward and forward toward the position for a high front vowel. The jaw is raised, and the lips become unrounded. See Figure 35.

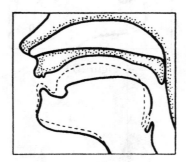

Figure 35

II. Examples

The examples that will now be presented illustrate the diphthongs just discussed. While listening to these examples, please keep in mind that in your own dialect these words may not be produced exactly as they are on the tape.

Turn on the tape recorder and follow along.

	Initial	*Medial*	*Final*
/eɪ/	ale aim	haze same assail	hay weigh
/oʊ/	old own	cold grown foam	mow dough
/aɪ/	eye iris	file height align	by imply
/aʊ/	out owl	clown renown announcer	now allow
/ɔɪ/	oyster oil	foil joyful boisterous	coy alloy

III.   Self-Test: Diphthongs

This self-test will assess your ability to recognize and transcribe diphthongs in both real and nonsense words. Also, it will give you an indication of what you will need to be able to do by the end of this laboratory session.

In the spaces provided, write the correct symbols for the diphthongs contained in the real words and nonsense words that will now be heard.

Start tape now.

Real words

1. _____   9. _____
2. _____   10. _____
3. _____   11. _____   _____
4. _____   12. _____   _____
5. _____   13. _____   _____
6. _____   14. _____   _____
7. _____   15. _____   _____
8. _____

Nonsense words

16. _____   _____   21. _____   _____
17. _____   _____   22. _____   _____
18. _____   _____   23. _____   _____
19. _____   _____   24. _____   _____
20. _____   _____   25. _____   _____

Check your answers in the back of this book.
- If you made only 2 (or fewer) errors, go directly to Exercise E. However, you may wish to do some of the earlier exercises for additional practice with diphthongs.
- If you made more than 2 errors, you will need to do all of the exercises in this part of Laboratory Session 5. Go directly to the first practice exercise.

IV.   Practice Exercises

The following exercises are graded in difficulty, with the later exercises being more difficult than the earlier ones. Work at your own pace, and write your answers in the appropriate spaces.

A.   *Yes-No Discriminations*

For each word that will now be heard, indicate whether or not it contains a *diphthong*.

Start tape now.

	+	−		+	−
1.	_____	_____	6.	_____	_____
2.	_____	_____	7.	_____	_____
3.	_____	_____	8.	_____	_____
4.	_____	_____	9.	_____	_____
5.	_____	_____	10.	_____	_____

Indicate whether or not each word that will now be heard contains an /aɪ/ diphthong.

	+	−		+	−
11.	_____	_____	14.	_____	_____
12.	_____	_____	15.	_____	_____
13.	_____	_____	16.	_____	_____

Indicate whether or not each word that will now be heard contains an /aɷ/ diphthong.

	+	−		+	−
17.	_____	_____	20.	_____	_____
18.	_____	_____	21.	_____	_____
19.	_____	_____	22.	_____	_____

Indicate whether or not each word that will now be heard contains an /ɔɪ/ diphthong.

	+	−		+	−
23.	_____	_____	26.	_____	_____
24.	_____	_____	27.	_____	_____
25.	_____	_____	28.	_____	_____

Check your answers in the back of this book. If you made more than 1 error, please repeat this exercise, paying particular attention to the items that gave you difficulty. If you made only 1 error (or no errors), go on to the next exercise.

B.   *Aural Only Presentation: Specific Positions*

The words that will now be heard contain diphthongs in specific positions. In each case, write the correct symbol for the diphthong that you hear in the space provided.

Start tape now.

Initial position

1. _____	6. _____
2. _____	7. _____
3. _____	8. _____
4. _____	9. _____
5. _____	10. _____

Medial position

11. _____	16. _____
12. _____	17. _____
13. _____	18. _____
14. _____	19. _____
15. _____	20. _____

Final position

21. _____	26. _____
22. _____	27. _____
23. _____	28. _____
24. _____	29. _____
25. _____	30. _____

Now check your answers in the back of this book. If you made more than 1 error, please repeat this exercise. If you made no errors, or only 1 error, go on to Exercise C.

C.   *Written and Aural Presentation: Combined Positions*

The words that will now be heard contain diphthongs in a variety of positions. In the spaces provided, write the correct symbols for the diphthongs that you hear.

Start tape now.

1.	_____	lonely	9.	_____		topsoil
2.	_____	doubtful	10.	_____		pound
3.	_____	turpentine	11.	_____	_____	housewife
4.	_____	mane	12.	_____	_____	hindsight
5.	_____	poised	13.	_____	_____	cowboy
6.	_____	final	14.	_____	_____	wayside
7.	_____	disarray	15.	_____	_____	loudmouth
8.	_____	although				

Now check your answers in the back of this book. If you made more than 1 error, please repeat this exercise. Otherwise, go on to Exercise D.

D.   *Aural Only Presentation: Combined Positions*

The words that will now be heard contain diphthongs in a variety of positions. In the spaces provided, write the correct symbols for the diphthongs that you hear.

Start tape now.

1.	_____	9.	_____	
2.	_____	10.	_____	_____
3.	_____	11.	_____	_____
4.	_____	12.	_____	_____
5.	_____	13.	_____	_____
6.	_____	14.	_____	_____
7.	_____	15.	_____	_____
8.	_____			

Go on to the next exercise.

E. Aural Only Presentation: Combined Positions—Nonsense Words

In the spaces provided, write the correct symbols for the diphthongs that you hear in these nonsense words.

Start tape now.

1. _____ _____   6. _____ _____

2. _____ _____   7. _____ _____

3. _____ _____   8. _____ _____

4. _____ _____   9. _____ _____

5. _____ _____   10. _____ _____

Now check your answers to these exercises in the back of this book. If you made more than 1 error on either exercise, please redo that exercise. If you made fewer than 2 errors on both of these exercises, you are ready to do the final exercise for Part B of this laboratory session.

F. Final Exercise: Diphthongs

In the spaces provided, write the correct symbols for the diphthongs contained in the real words and nonsense words that will now be heard.

Start tape now.

Real words

1. _____   9. _____

2. _____   10. _____

3. _____   11. _____ _____

4. _____   12. _____ _____

5. _____   13. _____ _____

6. _____   14. _____ _____

7. _____   15. _____ _____

8. _____

Nonsense words

16. _____ _____   19. _____ _____

17. _____ _____   20. _____ _____

18. _____ _____   21. _____ _____

Check your answers in the back of this book. If you missed more than 2 symbols, go back to the review of content and the examples given for Part B of this laboratory session. Then redo this exercise. If you made 0 to 2 errors, good work! You are ready to go on to the combined exercise on central vowels and diphthongs.

COMBINED EXERCISE: CENTRAL VOWELS AND DIPHTHONGS

In the spaces provided, write the correct symbols for the central vowels and diphthongs contained in the real words and nonsense words that will now be heard.

Start tape now.

Real words

1.	_____	_____		8.	_____	_____	
2.	_____	_____		9.	_____	_____	
3.	_____	_____		10.	_____	_____	_____
4.	_____	_____		11.	_____	_____	_____
5.	_____	_____		12.	_____	_____	_____
6.	_____	_____		13.	_____	_____	_____
7.	_____	_____		14.	_____	_____	_____

Nonsense words

15.	_____	_____		19.	_____	_____	_____
16.	_____	_____		20.	_____	_____	_____
17.	_____	_____		21.	_____	_____	_____
18.	_____	_____		22.	_____	_____	_____ _____

Check your answers to this exercise in the back of this book. If you made more than 3 errors, go back and review this laboratory session, focusing on the sounds that were difficult for you. If you made fewer than 4 errors, congratulations! You are ready to go on to the test for Laboratory Session 5.

TEST: CENTRAL VOWELS AND DIPHTHONGS

In the spaces provided, write the correct symbols for the central vowels and diphthongs contained in the real and nonsense words that will now be heard. To pass this laboratory session you will need to make no more than 2 errors on the real words and no more than 2 errors on the nonsense words.

Start tape now.

Real words

1. _____ _____   9. _____ _____

2. _____ _____   10. _____ _____

3. _____ _____   11. _____ _____ _____

4. _____ _____   12. _____ _____ _____

5. _____ _____   13. _____ _____ _____

6. _____ _____   14. _____ _____ _____ _____

7. _____ _____   15. _____ _____ _____ _____

8. _____ _____

Nonsense words

16. _____ _____   21. _____ _____

17. _____ _____   22. _____ _____ _____

18. _____ _____   23. _____ _____ _____

19. _____ _____   24. _____ _____ _____

20. _____ _____   25. _____ _____ _____ _____

Laboratory Review II
Consonants, Vowels, and Diphthongs

You have now covered all the consonant and vowel sounds of standard American English. This review will give you a chance to practice using all the symbols you have learned.

OBJECTIVES

- First, when presented with a spoken list of 14 real words containing a variety of consonants and vowels (including diphthongs), you will correctly transcribe all the sounds in those words with 95% accuracy.
- Second, while listening to 6 nonsense words containing a variety of consonants and vowels (including diphthongs), you will correctly transcribe all the sounds in those nonsense words with 90% accuracy.

LABORATORY REVIEW II

Practice Exercise A: Vowels and Diphthongs

In the spaces provided, write the correct symbols for the vowels and diphthongs contained in the real and nonsense words that will now be heard.

Start tape now.

Real words

1. _____ _____   14. _____ _____
2. _____ _____   15. _____ _____
3. _____ _____   16. _____ _____
4. _____ _____   17 _____ _____ _____
5. _____ _____   18. _____ _____ _____
6. _____ _____   19. _____ _____ _____
7. _____ _____   20. _____ _____ _____
8. _____ _____   21. _____ _____ _____
9. _____ _____   22. _____ _____ _____
10. _____ _____   23 _____ _____ _____
11. _____ _____   24. _____ _____ _____ _____
12. _____ _____   25. _____ _____ _____
13. _____ _____   26. _____ _____ _____ _____ _____

Nonsense words

27. _____ _____ _____   32. _____ _____ _____
28. _____ _____   33. _____ _____
29. _____ _____   34. _____ _____ _____
30. _____ _____ _____   35. _____ _____
31. _____ _____ _____   36. _____ _____ _____ _____

Check your answers in the back of this book. If you made more than 3 errors on either part, please repeat the exercise. Otherwise, go on to Practice Exercise B.

Practice Exercise B: Consonants, Vowels, and Diphthongs

In the spaces provided, write the correct symbols for the consonants and vowels (including diphthongs) that make up each real word and nonsense word that will now be heard. In some of the cases, the correct number of spaces is provided. In others, no individual spaces are given. Simply transcribe all the sounds that you hear. Enclose these whole-word transcriptions in virgules (slashes) to indicate that the words are transcribed broadly—that is, without narrow phonetic detail, as in /kæt/ for *cat*.

This exercise will give you a chance to put together everything you have learned thus far about phonetic transcription.

Start tape now.

Real words

1. _____ _____ _____ _____ _____ _____
2. _____ _____ _____ _____ _____ _____
3. _____ _____ _____ _____ _____ _____
4. _____ _____ _____ _____ _____ _____
5. _____ _____ _____ _____ _____ _____
6. _____ _____ _____ _____ _____ _____ _____
7. _____
8. _____
9. _____
10. _____
11. _____

Nonsense words

12. _____ _____ _____ _____ _____
13. _____ _____ _____ _____ _____
14. _____ _____ _____ _____ _____ _____ _____
15. _____
16. _____

Check your answers in the back of the book. If you made more than 7 errors, you should go back and review the appropriate laboratory sessions before taking the test that follows. If you made 0 to 7 errors, good job! Go on to the test.

TEST: CONSONANTS, VOWELS, AND DIPHTHONGS

The directions for this test are the same as those given for Practice Exercise B, just completed. The answers to this test are not in your workbook. Please turn in your test at the appropriate class meeting. To pass this test, you must make no more than 5 errors on the real words and 3 errors on the nonsense words.

Start tape now.

Real words

1. _____ _____ _____ _____ _____ _____
2. _____ _____ _____ _____ _____ _____
3. _____ _____ _____ _____ _____ _____
4. _____ _____ _____ _____ _____ _____ _____
5. _____ _____ _____ _____ _____ _____
6. _____ _____ _____ _____ _____ _____ _____
7. _____ _____ _____ _____ _____ _____ _____ _____ _____
8. _____
9. _____
10. _____
11. _____
12. _____
13. _____
14. _____

Nonsense words

15. _____ _____ _____ _____ _____
16. _____ _____ _____ _____ _____
17. _____ _____ _____ _____ _____ _____
18. _____
19. _____
20. _____

Laboratory Session 6
Diacritics

OBJECTIVES

In this laboratory session, you will learn to recognize certain types of sound modifications and to capture them in your transcriptions using diacritic markers. By the end of this session, you will be expected to meet the following specific objectives:

- First, when presented with a spoken list of 10 real words, you will completely transcribe those words, using diacritic markers whenever appropriate. The diacritics covered in this laboratory session will be used with 90% accuracy.
- Second, when presented with a spoken list of six nonsense words, you will completely transcribe those words, using the diacritic markers covered in this laboratory session with 90% accuracy.

AVERAGE TIME

1 3/4 hours (range: 40 minutes to 4 hours)

DIACRITICS

I. Review of Content

Diacritics or *diacritic markers* are special symbols that are added to consonant or vowel symbols to represent modifications of those sounds. Diacritics, which add phonetic detail, are required in *narrow* transcriptions, but not in *broad* transcriptions of the type you have been using.*

The International Phonetic Alphabet (IPA) includes many diacritics that are used to show slight modifications in place of articulation, manner of articulation, voicing, lip shape, tongue height, and so forth. Additional diacritics have been made up specifically for use in transcribing the speech of young children or individuals with speech disorders (e.g., see Bush et al., 1973, and Shriberg and Kent, 1982).

What follows is not an exhaustive list of all available diacritics, but a sample of several diacritics that are often used in narrow transcriptions of normal adult English (as well as in transcribing children's speech). Each one is explained briefly. A capital *C* or *V* is used simply to show the appropriate placement of each diacritic. The appendix contains a more extensive list of diacritics that are useful in transcribing children's or disordered speech.

C^h An aspirated stop (i.e., one followed by a "puff of air"). This applies to /p, t, k/ in English and occurs mainly before stressed vowels, as in [tʰaɪni] or [bɪkʰʌm]. (If only a small amount of aspiration is heard, the diacritic C' may be used.

$C =$ An unaspirated voiceless stop; in English, such stops occur primarily in /s/ + stop clusters, as in [sp=un] or [st=ɔp].

$C^\urcorner$ An unreleased stop. The articulators move into the appropriate position, but the stop seems to be "swallowed." This sometimes happens at the ends of words, as in [fit˺].

C_w A labialized consonant (i.e., one produced with lip rounding that is not normally a part of its production). Consonants are often labialized preceding labial consonants or round vowels in English, as in [twɪn] or [su].

$\tilde{V}$ A nasalized vowel (i.e., one produced without velic closure). Such vowels often occur just before nasal consonants in English, as in [fæ̃n].

---

*Note that narrow transcriptions are enclosed in square brackets ([ ]), whereas virgules or slashes (/ /) are used for broad transcriptions.

C, V	A sound that is normally voiced is produced without full voicing. This frequently happens at the ends of words in English, as in [noz] for *nose*. In addition, voiced sounds are often at least partially devoiced when they precede voiceless sounds as in [lɔbstɚ] for *lobster*.
C	A dentalized consonant (i.e., one produced with the tip or blade of the tongue touching the upper teeth). In English alveolar consonants are often dentalized when they precede dental consonants. For example, the /n/ in *tenth* is dentalized because of the following /θ/ (i.e., [tɛn̪θ]).
ɫ	A velarized consonant (i.e., one produced with the back of the tongue raised toward the velum). As pointed out in Laboratory Session 3, when /l/ follows a vowel, especially at the end of a word or before a word-final consonant, it is usually produced in this way. For example, the /l/ in *full* is a "dark" or velarized /l/, as is the /l/ in *bowls* (i.e.,[fʊɫ] and [boʊɫz].
C̩	A "syllabic" consonant (i.e., a liquid or nasal that functions like a vowel as the main part of a syllable). Examples include the /l/ in *bottle* [bɔtl̩] and the /n/ in *button* [bʌtn̩]. Generally, a syllabic consonant is produced with the same articulators as the immediately preceding consonant. That is, the two consonants are *homorganic*.

The examples and exercises in this laboratory session will focus on these nine diacritics. Because they are among the most frequently used diacritic markers, they should be mastered.

II. Examples

The examples that will now be heard illustrate the use of the nine diacritics just described.

Turn on the tape recorder and follow along.

	Initial	Medial	Final	Clusters
C^h	pig tough cage	upon attack decay	zip fat ache	plan creep lamp belt
$C^=$	—	aspire astound subscribe	—	spin stamp skirt
$C^˥$	—	—	zip fat bed lag	part lamp card
C_w	shoe cool rouge	—	—	swing twin thwart queen
$\tilde{V}$	under answer only	found dance pin	—	—
C_o	—	—	nose bed flag	cars bells lagged amazed
C_n	—	—	—	tenth width
ϵ	—	—	bowl dull owl	bolt felt milk
C_l	—	—	button middle paddle	mittens bottles tattles

III.   Self-Test: Diacritics

This self-test will assess your ability to recognize the sound modifications covered in this laboratory session and to capture them in your transcriptions of both real ånd nonsense words using diacritic markers. Also, it will give you an indication of what you should be able to do by the end of this laboratory session.

Completely transcribe the real and nonsense words that will now be heard, using the diacritics covered in this session whenever appropriate.

Start tape now.

Real words

1. _____   6. _____

2. _____   7. _____

3. _____   8. _____

4. _____   9. _____

5. _____   10. _____

Nonsense words

11. _____   14. _____

12. _____   15. _____

13. _____   16. _____

Check your answers in the back of this workbook.
- If you made 0 to 3 errors on diacritics, go directly to Exercise G. However, you may wish to do some of the earlier exercises for additional practice.
- If you made more than 3 errors on diacritics you will need to do all of the practice exercises in this laboratory session. Go directly to Exercise A.

IV.   Practice Exercises

The following exercises are graded in difficulty, with the last ones being harder than the first ones. Please complete all the practice exercises. Work at your own pace, and write your answers in the spaces provided.

A.   *Yes-No Discriminations*

You will now hear six real words. Indicate whether or not each contains an *aspirated stop.*

Start tape now.

	+	−		+	−
1.	_____	_____	4.	_____	_____
2.	_____	_____	5.	_____	_____
3.	_____	_____	6.	_____	_____

Indicate whether or not each word that will now be heard contains a *nasalized vowel.*

	+	−		+	−
7.	_____	_____	10.	_____	_____
8.	_____	_____	11.	_____	_____
9.	_____	_____	12.	_____	_____

Indicate whether or not each word that will now be heard contains a *velarized /l/.*

	+	−		+	−
13.	_____	_____	16.	_____	_____
14.	_____	_____	17.	_____	_____
15.	_____	_____	18.	_____	_____

Check your answers in the back of this book. If you missed more than 2 items, please repeat this exercise, paying close attention to the diacritics that gave you difficulty. If you missed only 2 (or fewer) items, go on to the next exercise.

B.   *Written and Aural Presentation: Specific Positions*

Transcribe the italicized sound in each word that will now be heard, using one or more of the diacritics discussed earlier in this session. If more than one diacritic marker is to be used, the appropriate number is given in parentheses after the word.

Start the tape now.

Initial position

1. _____   *a*nchor
2. _____   *k*in
3. _____   *t*imid
4. _____   *a*ny
5. _____   *p*ass
6. _____   *c*oo (2)

Medial position

7. _____   as*t*onish
8. _____   su*p*erb
9. _____   ba*n*ish
10. _____   fo*l*ding
11. _____   re*q*uire (2)
12. _____   fe*n*ce

Final position

13. _____   ca*t*
14. _____   fa*ll*
15. _____   lis*t*en
16. _____   atta*ck*
17. _____   tur*tle* (2)
18. _____   ro*s*e

Clusters

19. _____   s*p*in
20. _____   col*d*
21. _____   s*ch*ool (2)
22. _____   *q*ueen (2)
23. _____   be*lt*
24. _____   *q*uill (2)

Check your answers in the back of the book. If you missed more than 3 items, please repeat this exercise. Otherwise, go on to Exercise C.

C. *Aural Only Presentation: Specific Positions*

Each word that will now be heard contains a sound, in the specified position, that should be transcribed using one or more of the diacritics covered in this laboratory session. Transcribe the specified sound, using all appropriate diacritics. If more than one diacritic is to be used, the number is given in parentheses.

Start the tape now.

Initial position

1. _____
2. _____
3. _____
4. _____ (2)
5. _____
6. _____

Final position

13. _____
14. _____
15. _____
16. _____
17. _____
18. _____ (2)

Medial position

7. _____ /t/ (2)
8. _____ /l/
9. _____ /t/ (2)
10. _____ /æ/
11. _____ /p/
12. _____ /k/

Clusters

19. _____ /t/
20. _____ /p/
21. _____ /k/ (2)
22. _____ /t/ (2)
23. _____ /s/
24. _____ /k/

Check your answers in the back of this book. If you made more than 3 errors, please repeat this exercise. If you made 0 to 3 errors, go on to Exercise D.

D. Written and Aural Presentation: Combined Positions

Transcribe the italicized sounds in each word that will now be heard, using one or more of the diacritics covered in this laboratory session. If more than one diacritic is to be used for one sound, the appropriate number is given in parentheses after the word.

Start tape now.

1. _____   *c*ube (2)   9. _____ _____   mis*ta*ke

2. _____ _____ *t*a*p*   10. _____ _____   *ca*ne

3. _____ _____ *po*se   11. _____ _____   s*t*ark

4. _____   bee*tle* (2)   12. _____   hus*tle* (2)

5. _____   defea*t*   13. _____ _____ _____ *can't*

6. _____   fu*ll*   14. _____ _____   *pi*ll

7. _____   woo*d*en   15. _____ _____ _____ s*ti*nk

8. _____ _____ s*wa*m

Check your answers to this exercise in the back of the book. If you made more than 2 errors, please repeat this exercise. If you made 0 to 2 errors, go on to Exercise E.

E. Written and Aural Presentation: Combined Positions—Whole Words

Transcribe the 10 words that will now be heard in their entirety, using the diacritics presented in this laboratory session. The correct number of spaces is given for each word, and the sounds that should be transcribed narrowly are italicized.

1. _____ _____ _____ _____   mus*cle*

2. _____ _____ _____ _____   *camp*

3. _____ _____ _____ _____   *s*tone

4. _____ _____ _____   lo*v*e

5. _____ _____ _____ _____   *swi*m

6. _____ _____ _____ _____   *sp*oon

7. _____ _____ _____ _____   thi*nk*

8. _____ _____ _____ _____ _____   *qui*lt

9. _____ _____ _____   *po*ise

10. _____ _____ _____ _____ _____ _____   s*parkle*

Check your answers in the back of this book. If you made 4 or more errors, please repeat this exercise, paying close attention to the sounds that gave you difficulty. If you made fewer than 4 errors, go on to Exercise F.

F. *Aural Only Presentation: Combined Positions—Whole Words (With Spaces)*

Completely transcribe the 16 real and nonsense words that will now be heard, using the diacritics covered in this laboratory session whenever appropriate. The correct number of spaces is given for each word.

Start tape now.

Real words

1. __ __ __ __   6. __ __ __ __ __
2. __ __ __ __ __ __   7. __ __ __ __ __
3. __ __ __ __   8. __ __ __ __ __ __
4. __ __ __ __ __ __   9. __ __ __ __ __ __ __ __
5. __ __ __ __   10. __ __ __ __

Nonsense words

11. __ __ __ __ __   14. __ __ __ __
12. __ __ __ __ __   15. __ __ __ __
13. __ __ __ __   16. __ __ __ __

Check your answers in the back of this book. If you made 5 or more errors on diacritics, repeat this exercise, paying close attention to the diacritics that you missed. If you made fewer than 5 errors, go on to Exercise G.

(Note: You should have made no more than 4 errors on the consonants and vowels in this exercise.)

G. Aural Only Presentation: Combined Positions—Whole Words (Without Spaces)

Completely transcribe the 16 real and nonsense words that will now be heard, using the diacritics covered in this laboratory session whenever appropriate to modify the segmental symbols. In this exercise, no individual spaces are provided. Transcribe each word in its entirety on the line that is given. Enclose the transcription for each word in brackets ([ ]) to indicate that it is a narrow transcription.

Start tape now.

Real words

1. _____   6. _____

2. _____   7. _____

3. _____   8. _____

4. _____   9. _____

5. _____   10. _____

Nonsense words

11. _____   14. _____

12. _____   15. _____

13. _____   16. _____

Check your answers in the back of this book. If you made 5 or more errors on diacritics, go back to the review of content and the examples for this laboratory session, focusing on the diacritics that were a problem for you. If you made 0 to 4 errors, congratulations! You are ready to take the test for this laboratory session.

(Note: You should have made no more than 4 errors on the consonants and vowels in this exercise.)

TEST: DIACRITICS

Completely transcribe the real and nonsense words that will now be heard, using the diacritics covered in this laboratory session whenever appropriate. To pass this test and the laboratory session, you should make no more than 3 diacritic errors on the real words and 1 diacritic error on the nonsense words. (You should also make no more than 4 errors on the consonants and vowels contained in these 16 real and nonsense words.) Enclose the transcription of each word in brackets ([ ]).

Real words

1. _____
2. _____
3. _____
4. _____
5. _____

6. _____
7. _____
8. _____
9. _____
10. _____

Nonsense words

11. _____
12. _____
13. _____

14. _____
15. _____
16. _____

Laboratory Session 7
Suprasegmentals

In this laboratory session you will learn to recognize and transcribe suprasegmentals or prosodic features (i.e., stress, intonation, and length). However, the scope of this course does not permit going into depth on all of these suprasegmentals. Because of the importance of stress in English, we have chosen to focus on stress in this laboratory session; intonation and length will be covered in less detail. In the test for Laboratory Review III, you will be responsible for marking word stress. In fact, word stress should be marked in all of your transcriptions from now on.

OBJECTIVES

By the end of this lab, you will be expected to meet three specific objectives:

- First, when presented with a spoken list of 10 words containing more than one syllable, you will use diacritic markers to correctly indicate the stress pattern of each word with 95% accuracy.
- Second, when presented with a spoken list of 15 simple sentences, you will select the appropriate intonation pattern from the choices given with 95% accuracy.
- Third, when presented with 16 pairs of real or nonsense words, in which the members of each pair differ only in the length of one segment, you will correctly indicate which member of the pair has the lengthened segment and will transcribe that member with 95% accuracy, using the appropriate diacritic for length.

AVERAGE TIME (Including Laboratory Review III)

2½ hours (range: 1 hour to 4 hours)

Note: Because this is a long laboratory session, consisting of three parts, you may not want to do it all at once. However, the test at the end covers all three parts.

SUPRASEGMENTALS

Overview

Suprasegmentals or *prosodic features* are said to be "superimposed on" or "distributed over" strings of segments (Lehiste, 1970). That is, the "domain" of a suprasegmental is generally larger than one segment. For example, it may be an entire syllable or word. Where suprasegmentals are concerned, comparisons or relative values are crucial. For instance, to decide if a vowel is long (i.e., lengthened), it is necessary to compare its length to that of another vowel. Suprasegmentals are also complicated because they may interact or influence one another. For example, stressed vowels in English tend to be longer than unstressed vowels; thus stress and length often interact.

The three suprasegmentals covered in this lab have different functions in the linguistic system of English. *Length* is not "significant" in English, but rather is largely predictable, depending, for example, on neighboring sounds. On the other hand, *stress* is very important because stress differences are sometimes used to distinguish words containing the same sounds—for example, *convict* (noun) versus *convict* (verb).

Intonation also serves an important function in English because the meaning of a phrase or sentence may depend crucially on its intonation pattern. For instance, the two words "You're going" mean quite different things depending on the intonation. Compare "You're going." (statement) versus "You're going!" (exclamation) versus "You're going?" (question). Note that to some extent punctuation provides a visual representation of intonation.

PART A

STRESS

I. Review of Content

A stressed syllable is said to be produced with extra force or increased muscular effort. A stressed or accented syllable is heard as being louder and clearer than an unstressed syllable. The sounds in stressed syllables are pronounced more clearly and more precisely; the vowels are longer and more distinct and are less likely to be centralized or reduced. Unstressed vowels, on the other hand, are likely to be pronounced as [ə] or [ɪ], as in the second and fourth syllables of *demonstration*. In longer words it is often possible to discern two or more degrees of stress.

Stress can be marked with accent marks, ´ for primary, ` for secondary, and ˆ for tertiary. Shriberg and Kent (1982) use numbers (1, 2, and 3) written just above the "nucleus" of the syllable (usually a vowel) to show three degrees of stress. In the IPA system (1978), small vertical lines are placed to the left of stressed syllables. For syllables with primary stress, the small vertical line is placed above and to the left of the first symbol of the stressed syllable. For secondary stress, the line is placed just below and to the left of the first symbol of the syllable. For example, the word *leprechaun* would be transcribed as follows: [ˈlɛprɪˌkʰɑn]. The IPA system is sometimes difficult to use because it necessitates knowing where syllable boundaries fall. Therefore, in this laboratory session the traditional system will be used; accent marks will be placed over vowels to represent primary and secondary stress. Tertiary stress will not be marked.

Stress or prominence is a very important part of English, as noted earlier. English has "free" stress. That is, different syllables may be accented. Thus, speakers must derive rules for assigning stress (Klein, 1984). Stress assignment in English is very complicated and depends on many factors (e.g., see Chomsky and Halle, 1968). Although it is not actually possible to predict which syllable of a word will be stressed, some general statements can be made. For example, Prator and Robinett (1972) discuss the following guidelines:

1. In most two-syllable words, the stress is on the first syllable (e.g., *Túesday, dínner, Ápril, chícken, thúnder*).
2. In compound nouns, the first part of the compound generally receives the primary stress, and the second part receives secondary stress, as in *cówbòy, dóorknòb, bláckmàil,* and *Súpermàn*. Sometimes, both parts of a compound may appear to have primary stress (Shriberg and Kent, 1982). Such words are called *spondees* (e.g., *gráybéard*).
3. Compound verbs generally have secondary stress on the first element and primary stress on the second element (e.g., *ùnderstánd, òvercóme, òversée*).
4. Two-syllable pronouns usually have main stress on the second syllable, as in *mysélf, yoursélves*.
5. Many words of Latin origin have primary stress on the first syllable when they are used as nouns and primary stress on the second syllable when they are used as verbs (e.g., *insert, protest, permit*). (The vowel differences that occur are considered to result from the differences in stress.)
6. The stress of a word usually does not change when a suffix is added (e.g., *háppy, háppiness, háppily, háppier*). However, words that end in certain suffixes such as *-tion, -ic, -ical,* and *-ity* generally have primary stress on the syllable preceding the suffix, as in *translátion, heróic, publícity*.

The stress pattern of a multisyllabic word is not predictable in English. For example, a three syllable word may have only one stress, as in *sýmpathy* (í-2-3) and *renéwal* (1-2́-3), or it may have two stresses, as in *gùarantée* (ì-2-3́).* Similarly, a four-syllable word may have only one stress, as in *áccuracy* (í-2-3-4) or *apólogy* (1-2́-3-4), or it may have two stresses, as in *èvolútion* (ì-2-3́-4). Longer words generally have more than one stress, as in *apòlogétic* (1-2̀-3-4́-5), but they may have just one stress—for example, *abólishable* (1-2́-3-4-5).

In addition to word stress, *sentence stress* is also an important feature of English. In phrases and sentences, some words are stressed more than others. The words that are stressed are typically *content words,* such as nouns and verbs. *Function words,* for example, articles and prepositions, are not usually stressed. Stressed words are said more slowly and are more distinct and more precisely articulated. When sentence stress falls on a word containing more than one syllable, it falls on the syllable that is normally stressed, as in, "I'll sée you tomórrow" (Prator and Robinett, 1972). In English, sentence stresses tend to occur at regular intervals, so English is said to be a "stress-timed" language. Some word stresses are dropped, and words that are not stressed tend to be "compressed" and said more rapidly. Compare, for example, "The bóy búilds mány módels" and "The bóy is ínterested in constrúcting módels." Although sentence stress is important in English, because of time limitations we will cover only word stress in this laboratory session.

---

*Following Prator and Robinett (1972), the numerals 1, 2, 3, and so forth, are used to represent the number of syllables in a word. Accent marks placed above these numerals indicate which syllables are stressed.

II. Examples

The following examples illustrate some common stress patterns that characterize words with two, three, four, and five syllables.

Two-syllable words

í-2	1-2́	í-2̀	ì-2́	í-2̀	1-2́
márry	abóut	gréenhoùse	mỳsélf	cóndùct	condúct
júdgment	becóme	drúgstòre	hìmsélf	súspèct	suspéct
láter	secúre	séagùll	yòursélves	pérmìt	permít
				rébel	rebél

Three-syllable words

í-2-3	1-2́-3	ì-2-3́
háppiness	extínguish	prèmatúre
énergy	malícious	àscertáin
ámbulance	delíver	òvercóme

Four-syllable words

í-2-3̀-4	1-2́-3-4	ì-2-3́-4	1-2́-3-4̀
délicacy	apólogy	èducátion	negótiàte
mémorable	attáinable	còntribútion	apólogìze
áccuracy	matérial	àbolítion	eléctrifỳ

Five-syllable words

ì-2-3́-4-5	1-2̀-3-4́-5
ìndetérminate	negòtiátion
àbolítionist	apòlogétic
ànnivérsary	commùnicátion

III. Practice Exercises

A. *Two-Syllable Words: One Stress*

The two-syllable words that will be heard have just one stress. There is no secondary stress. Mark the stress by placing an accent mark above the nucleus (vowel) of the stressed syllable.

Start tape now.

1. sofa
2. assume
3. carry
4. allow
5. align
6. instant
7. youthful
8. subdue
9. destroy
10. minor
11. disease
12. placard

B. *Two-Syllable Words: Two Stresses*

The following two-syllable words have two stresses, a primary stress and a secondary stress. Mark the stressed vowels by placing accent marks above the appropriate letters.

1. postpone
2. convict
3. ozone
4. blackout
5. yourself
6. storehouse
7. sixteen
8. drugstore
9. himself
10. incline

Check your answers to these exercises in the back of this book. If you made any errors, please repeat the exercise. Otherwise go on to Exercise C.

C.   *Three-Syllable Words: One Stress*

The three-syllable words that will now be heard have only one stress, on either the first or the second syllable. Mark the stress by placing an accent mark directly over the stressed vowel.

Start tape now.

1. emphasis
2. enjoyment
3. eviction
4. abandon
5. vigilance
6. delicious
7. distinguish
8. emptiness
9. familiar
10. similar

D.   *Three-Syllable Words: Two Stresses*

Each three-syllable word that will now be heard has two stresses. The stress patterns that are represented are í-2-3̃ and ì-2-3́. Mark the primary and secondary stresses by placing accent marks directly above the appropriate vowel symbols.

Start tape now.

1. understand
2. weather vane
3. overlook
4. sacrifice
5. introduce
6. magnify
7. entertain
8. memorize
9. overcoat
10. evermore

Check your answers to these exercises in the back of this book. If you made more than 1 error, please repeat the exercise. Otherwise, go on to Exercise E.

E.   Four-Syllable Words

The four-syllable words that will now be heard have either one or two stresses. The stress patterns that are represented are 1́-2-3-4, 1-2́-3-4, and 1́-2-3́-4. Mark the stresses by placing accent marks above the appropriate letters.

Start tape now.

1. situation
2. demolition
3. philosophy
4. charismatic
5. conflagration
6. negotiable
7. democracy
8. amicably
9. scientific
10. additional

Check your answers in the back of this book. If you made any errors, repeat this exercise. If you made no errors, go on to Exercise F.

F.   Five-Syllable Words

Each five-syllable word that will now be heard has two stresses, a primary stress and a secondary stress. The stress patterns that are represented are 1́-2-3́-4-5 and 1-2́-3-4́-5. Mark the stress pattern of each word by placing the appropriate accent marks over the stressed vowels.

Start tape now.

1. philosophical
2. hypocritical
3. pronunciation
4. deliberation
5. nationality
6. biological
7. appropriation
8. antithetical
9. homogeneous
10. insurmountable

Check your answers in the back of this book. If you made any errors, please repeat the exercise. If you made no errors, go on to the final exercise for this part of Laboratory Session 7.

G.   *Final Exercise: Word Stress*

The words with two, three, and four syllables that will now be heard exemplify a variety of stress patterns. Some have only one stress, and others have both a primary and a secondary stress. Mark the stressed syllables by placing accent marks above the appropriate vowel symbols.

Start tape now.

1. blacktop
2. danger
3. sanity
4. friendlier
5. catastrophe
6. zoological

7. locate
8. construct
9. destroyer
10 direction
11 egocentric
12 appropriation

Check your answers in the back of this book. If you made any errors, please repeat this exercise. If you made no errors, good job! Go on to the next part of this laboratory session.

PART B

INTONATION

I.   Review of Content

As noted earlier, intonation is important in English. *Intonation* refers to the function of *pitch* or *vocal fold vibration* or *fundamental frequency* at the phrase or sentence level (Lehiste, 1970). We can control the rate of vibration of our vocal folds to some extent by controlling the rate of airflow across the glottis and the muscular tension in the vocal folds. Hence, we can control the pitch of our voices. Intonation involves the use of pitch changes to signal meaning differences in phrases and sentences. By changing the intonation pattern of an utterance, we can change the meaning of that utterance, although the meanings of the individual words do not change. So, intonation refers to patterns or contours of pitch changes that carry meaning (MacKay, 1978). In writing, intonation differences are sometimes represented by punctuation marks. For instance, compare "He's here!" to "He's here?"

Tone refers to the use of pitch differences at the word level. Some languages, such as Chinese, use tone as an important part of their linguistic system. Two (or more) words may be made up of exactly the same segments (consonants and vowels) but may have quite different meanings. These meaning differences are conveyed by different pitches or tones (e.g., high, low, rising, falling). To illustrate, [ma] said with a low tone might have a completely different meaning than [ma] said with a high tone. Tone is not part of the linguistic system of English, but intonation is. Therefore, this part of Laboratory Session 7 will focus on intonation.

Although much could be said about intonation, here we are covering only the intonation patterns that are characteristic of statements (as well as requests and commands) and questions. Only simple sentences are discussed. For complex sentences, each phrase or clause may have its own intonation contour. (For more information, see Pike, 1946.)

Statements, requests, commands, and *wh-questions* (i.e., questions that begin with words such as *who, where, when, what, why*) are generally said to have a "2 3 1" intonation pattern or contour (Grate, 1974). The pitch of the voice stays on a mid level (level 2) until the main sentence stress. At that point, the pitch of the voice rises to a level 3. It then falls to a lower level (level 1) and stays on that level until the end of the phrase. If one or more syllables follow the stress, the pitch "steps" down, but if the last syllable carries the stress, the pitch "glides" down (Grate, 1974). Compare, for example, "We híd it" (step-down) and "We híd" (glide-down). Exclamations are similar to statements except that the pitch rises even higher at the stress, and there is a sharper drop at the end.

Unlike wh-questions, questions requiring a "yes" or "no" answer (yes-no questions) are signaled by a rising intonation contour. The pitch of the voice begins at a mid level (level 2) and then rises to a level 3 at the last stress. It stays on level 3 until the last syllable, when there is a slight additional rise—for example, "Did they cóme?" (Grate, 1974).

Tag questions, attached to statements, are also frequently characterized by this rising intonation contour, as in "He left, didn't he?" However, tag questions may also be said as statements. In that case, there is a step down from level 3 to level 1—for example, "He left, didn't he."

II. Examples

The following examples illustrate a few common intonation patterns of American English. The system used to represent these intonation patterns is that of N.G. Grate (1974).

Statements

"step-down"

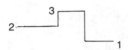

We híd it.
John might sée us.
He just returned from a méeting.

"glide-down"

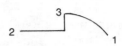

We híd.
John might sée.
He just returned from a tríp.

Wh-questions

"step-down"

Where's my súitcase?

Who is his bróther?

When's the párty?

"glide-down"

Where's my súit?

Who is hé?

When's the dánce?

Yes-no questions

Did they cóme?   Can you go wíth us?   Are you ángry?

Tag questions

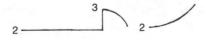

You don't want to gó, dó you?

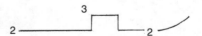

They haven't séen him, háve they?

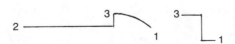

You don't want to gó, dó you?

They haven't séen him, háve they?

III.   Practice Exercises

A.   *Statements and Wh-Questions*

You will now hear seven simple sentences, each of which will be said twice. Each one has a 2 3 1 intonation contour, with the pitch either stepping down (A) or gliding down (B) after the main stress, which is already marked for you. In the spaces provided, write A or B to indicate which 2 3 1 intonation contour is correct for each sentence.

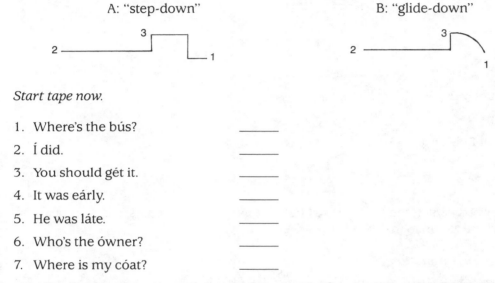

Start tape now.

1. Where's the bús?   _____

2. Í did.   _____

3. You should gét it.   _____

4. It was eárly.   _____

5. He was láte.   _____

6. Who's the ówner?   _____

7. Where is my cóat?   _____

Check your answers at the end of the book. If you made any errors, please repeat this exercise. Otherwise, go on to the next exercise.

B. Wh-Questions and Yes-No Questions

You will now hear six questions. In the spaces provided, write A, B, or C to indicate which intonation contour of the three given below is correct for each question. Remember that wh-questions have a *falling* intonation contour after the main stress, while yes/no questions have a *rising* intonation contour.

A: "rising"   B: "step-down"   C: "glide-down"

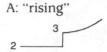   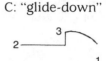

Start tape now.

1. Which man is your fáther?   _____

2. Who just came ín?   _____

3. Is that Súsan?   _____

4. Have you met Bób?   _____

5. How ís she?   _____

6. Who is thát?   _____

Check your answers in the back of the book. If you made any errors, please repeat this exercise. Otherwise, go on to the next exercise.

C. Final Exercise: Intonation

You will now hear eight simple statements and questions. Each is phonetically transcribed for you. Over each sentence draw the appropriate intonation pattern, selected from the three given below.

A: "rising"   B: "step-down"   C: "glide-down"

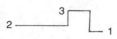   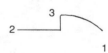

Start tape now.

1. [ʌɛr dɪd hi góʊ]   Where did he gó?

2. [hu ɪz wɪð ju]   Who is wíth you?

3. [ɪz ðɪs máɪn]   Is this míne?

4. [hɪɚ ðeɪ kʰʌm]   Here they cóme.

5. [haʊ ɑr wi gɛtɪŋ ðɛr]   How are we gétting there?

6. [ɑr ju háŋgri]   Are you húngry?

7. [hiz lóst]   He's lóst.

8. [ɪz kʰlæs óvɚ]   Is class óver?

Check your answers in the back of this book. If you made any errors, please repeat this exercise. Otherwise, go on to the next part of Laboratory Session 7.

PART C

LENGTH

I. Review of Content

Duration refers to the amount of time that a sound lasts. *Length* is perceived duration, and *quantity* refers to the use of length in a language (Lehiste, 1970) English does not use length as a significant part of its linguistic system, as do some languages (e.g., Polish, Italian, and Finnish). However, length differences do exist in English. For instance, low vowels are generally somewhat longer than high vowels, fricatives are longer than stops, and alveolars are shorter than most other consonants. Flaps and taps are the shortest consonants.

In English, vowels often differ in length depending on the following consonant. Vowels are measurably longer before voiced consonants than before similar voiceless consonants. Likewise, vowels are longer before fricatives than before similar stops (Lehiste, 1970). So, for instance, the /i/ vowel in *seed* is measurably (and perceptibly) longer than the same vowel in *seat*. Stress also influences duration in that stressed vowels tend to be longer and more distinct than unstressed vowels.

In a narrow transcription, length is represented by placing a colon (:) directly after the symbol for the segment (consonant or vowel) that is lengthened. If a sound is slightly lengthened, one dot may be placed after the appropriate symbol and above the line (e.g., V•). However, in this laboratory session, a colon will be used to represent any degree of length.

II. Examples

The first examples that will now be heard illustrate length differences in vowels that are due to the voicing quality of the following consonant. The second set of examples contains minimal pairs of nonsense words that differ only in the length of a specific consonant or vowel.

Turn on the tape recorder and follow along.

Real words		*Nonsense words*	
[sit]	[si:d]	[rɑmə]	[rɑ:mə]
[lus]	[lu:z]	[lete]	[le:te]
[mʌt]	[mʌ:d]	[al:o]	[al:o]
[sis]	[si:z]	[noto]	[not:o]
[rop]	[ro:b]	[ane]	[an:e]

III.   Practice Exercises

A.   *Length Discrimination*

For each pair of simple words that will now be heard, the vowel in one member of the pair is longer than the vowel in the other member. Circle the word in each pair that has the longer vowel. Each pair of words will be said twice.

Start tape now.

1.	bead	beat		4.	kiss	kit
2.	suit	sued		5.	buck	bug
3.	match	Madge		6.	maid	mate

Check your answers in the back of this book. If you made any errors, look at the review of content again and redo this exercise. If you made no errors, please go on.

B.   *Written and Aural Presentation: Real Words*

For each pair of real words that will now be heard, the vowel in one member of the pair is longer than the vowel in the other member. After deciding which word has the longer vowel, transcribe that word in the space provided. Indicate length by placing a colon after the appropriate symbol. If a diphthong is lengthened, place the length marker after the first element of the diphthong—for example, [a:ɪ].

Start tape now.

1.	bit	bid	_____	5.	log	lock	_____
2.	faze	face	_____	6.	mat	mass	_____
3.	mop	mob	_____	7.	"H"	age	_____
4.	moot	moose	_____	8.	Bert	bird	_____

Check your answers in the back of this book. If you made any errors, repeat the exercise. Otherwise, go on to Exercise C.

C. Written and Aural Presentation: Nonsense Words

Several pairs of nonsense words will now be heard. In each case, one segment will be considerably longer than the corresponding segment in the other member of the pair. After deciding which member of the pair has the lengthened segment, modify either the first or second broad transcription by placing a colon after the symbol representing the lengthened segment.

Start tape now.

	A	B		A	B
1.	/t u l i/	/t u l i/	5.	/b e n e/	/b e n e/
2.	/m o l o/	/m o l o/	6.	/s u m ə/	/s u m ə/
3.	/g ɑ t o/	/g ɑ t o/	7.	/t ɑ s o/	/t ɑ s o/
4.	/b ɝ l e/	/b ɝ l e/	8.	/s o v e/	/s o v e/

Check your answers in the back of this book. If you made any errors, please repeat the exercise. Otherwise, go on to Exercise D.

D. Aural Only Presentation: Real and Nonsense Words

First, three pairs of real words will be heard. Then three pairs of nonsense words will be heard. In each case, circle either the A or the B to indicate which member of the pair has the longer vowel. Then transcribe just that member of the pair, using a diacritic marker to indicate length.

Start tape now.

1.	A	B	_____	4.	A	B	_____
2.	A	B	_____	5.	A	B	_____
3.	A	B	_____	6.	A	B	_____

Check your answers in the back of this book. If you made any errors, please repeat this exercise. If you made no errors, congratulations! You are ready to go on to the test for this laboratory session.

TEST: SUPRASEGMENTALS

Stress

Mark the stress in the words of two, three, and four syllables that will now be heard by placing accent marks over the appropriate vowel symbols.

Start tape now.

1. warehouse
2. apple
3. utterance
4. immediate
5. nationality

6. suspend
7. undertake
8. disturbance
9. situation
10. enunciation

Intonation

Fifteen simple sentences (statements and questions) will now be heard. For each sentence, indicate whether the intonation pattern is 2 3 1 "step-down" (A), 2 3 1 "glide-down" (B), or 2 3 "rising" (C).

Start tape now.

1. Which man is your father? _____
2. Who just came in? _____
3. Please come in. _____
4. Have you met Jim? _____
5. They're living in Syracuse. _____
6. Did you finish your assignment? _____
7. Where does she live? _____

8. How do we get there? _____
9. Did you pass the test? _____
10. Can you see the sign? _____
11. Where's my ticket? _____
12. They're living in Rome. _____
13. It was early. _____
14. When is your birthday? _____
15. Who went to the party? _____

Length

Sixteen pairs of real or nonsense words will now be heard. In each case, one member of the pair differs from the other by having one segment that is noticeably longer than the corresponding segment in the other member. Circle A or B to indicate which member of the pair has the lengthened segment. Then transcribe only that member of the pair, using the appropriate diacritic for length.

Start tape now.

Real words

1.	A	B	_____	6.	A	B	_____
2.	A	B	_____	7.	A	B	_____
3.	A	B	_____	8.	A	B	_____
4.	A	B	_____	9.	A	B	_____
5.	A	B	_____	10.	A	B	_____

Nonsense words

11.	A	B	_____	14.	A	B	_____
12.	A	B	_____	15.	A	B	_____
13.	A	B	_____	16.	A	B	_____

Laboratory Review III
Consonants, Vowels, Diphthongs, and Diacritics

OBJECTIVES

- First, when presented with a spoken list of 18 real words, you will correctly transcribe all the consonants and vowels in those words with 95% accuracy; diacritics, including stress markers, will be used with 90% accuracy.
- Second, when presented with a spoken list of 10 nonsense words, you will narrowly transcribe those nonsense words with 90% accuracy, using all appropriate diacritics, including stress markers.

PRACTICE EXERCISE: CONSONANTS, VOWELS, DIPHTHONGS, AND DIACRITICS

This exercise will give you a chance to put together almost everything you have learned about transcription thus far. In the spaces provided, completely transcribe each real and nonsense word that will now be heard, using the diacritics covered in Laboratory Session 6 when appropriate, and marking primary and secondary stress as instructed in Laboratory Session 7. Enclose these "narrow" transcriptions in brackets ([ ]).

Each word will be said three times. After you hear the first production, turn off the tape and transcribe as much of the word as possible. After the second production, transcribe the rest of the consonants and vowels, and after the third production, add all appropriate diacritics, including stress markers.

Start tape now.

Real Words

1. _____   9. _____
2. _____   10. _____
3. _____   11. _____
4. _____   12. _____
5. _____   13. _____
6. _____   14. _____
7. _____   15. _____
8. _____   16. _____

Nonsense words

17. _____   21. _____
18. _____   22. _____
19. _____   23. _____
20. _____   24. _____

Check your answers in the back of this book. If you made more than 15 errors, repeat this exercise, paying close attention to the words or sounds that were difficult for you. If you made 0 to 15 errors, good work. Go on to the test for Laboratory Review III.

TEST: LABORATORY REVIEW III

The directions for this test are the same as those given for the practice exercise. Again, you are to completely transcribe the real and nonsense words in the spaces provided. Each word will be said three times.

Start tape now.

Real words

1. _____
2. _____
3. _____
4. _____
5. _____
6. _____
7. _____
8. _____
9. _____

10. _____
11. _____
12. _____
13. _____
14. _____
15. _____
16. _____
17. _____
18. _____

Nonsense words

19. _____
20. _____
21. _____
22. _____
23. _____

24. _____
25. _____
26. _____
27. _____
28. _____

Answers: Laboratory Session 1
Oral and Nasal Stop Consonants

ORAL STOP CONSONANTS

III.   Self-Test

Real words

1.	b	g		(brag)	6.	k	p	k	k	(cupcake)
2.	t	p		(temper)	7.	k	t			(squirt)
3.	g	t		(elegant)	8.	p	d			(paddle)
4.	b	b		(baseball)	9.	d	t	d		(doted)
5.	t	p	t	(toothpaste)	10.	g	t			(ghost)

Nonsense words

11.	k	d	k	(/kwæmdok/)	15.	g	p	t	(/glæplənt/)
12.	b	g	p	(/bɪnglɪp/)	16.	d	k	g	(/duskug/)
13.	p	t	k	(/pitkæŋ/)	17.	t	b		(/tɛmsɔb/)
14.	b	t		(/bræmɛt/)	18.	g	b	d	(/gibod/)

IV.   Practice Exercises

A.   Yes-No Discriminations

Oral stops

	+	−			+	−	
1.	x	—	(/bæ/)	7.	x	—	(/ip/)
2.	—	x	(/in/)	8.	—	x	(/æf/)
3.	x	—	(/tɔ/)	9.	x	—	(/ute/)
4.	x	—	(/dɔɪ/)	10.	—	x	(/ɪʃ/)
5.	—	x	(/sæ/)	11.	—	x	(/ʒo/)
6.	—	x	(/ʌvo/)	12.	x	—	(/ógi/)

Voiced oral stops

	+	−			+	−	
13.	x	—	(/abi/)	18.	x	—	(/dɪs/)
14.	—	x	(/tæʃ/)	19.	—	x	(/ðɪp/)
15.	x	—	(/geɪs/)	20.	—	x	(/kɑf/)
16.	—	x	(/ipɑ/)	21.	x	—	(/ugi/)
17.	—	x	(/nʌʒ/)	22.	x	—	(dɑb/)

Velar stops

	+	−			+	−	
23.	x	—	(/agi/)	27.	x	—	(koɒ/)
24.	x	—	(/ɛki/)	28.	—	x	(/moz/)
25.	—	x	(/tip/)	29.	—	x	(/mido/)
26.	—	x	(/ibɪn/)	30.	x	—	(/boge/)

B.   Aural Only Presentation: Specific Positions

Initial position   *Final position*

1.	b	(boulder)	13.	g	(brogue)
2.	d	(dependable)	14.	b	(bathtub)
3.	p	(polish)	15.	p	(regroup)
4.	d	(doily)	16.	t	(erudite)
5.	t	(Thomas)	17.	k	(dynamic)
6.	k	(camel)	18.	d	(renegade)
7.	p	(penicillin)	19.	p	(envelope)
8.	g	(gasp)	20.	g	(renege)
9.	b	(believable)	21.	d	(injured)
10.	k	(committee)	22.	b	(innertube)
11.	t	(tambourine)	23.	k	(picnic)
12.	g	(guarantee)	24.	t	(fought)

Medial position   *Initial Clusters*   *Final Clusters*

25.	p	(deeply)	37.	t	(twinkle)	49.	t	(carts)
26.	t	(batting)	38.	k	(cringe)	50.	b	(rhubarb)
27.	b	(ember)	39.	p	(plumber)	51.	g	(morgue)
28.	k	(slinky)	40.	g	(grand)	52.	d	(toward)
29.	p	(supper)	41.	b	(brunette)	53.	p	(clasp)
30.	d	(madly)	42.	d	(dwindle)	54.	k	(embark)
31.	g	(ignorant)	43.	k	(squirm)	55.	p	(lamp)
32.	d	(advent)	44.	p	(spring)	56.	g	(figs)
33.	k	(boxer)	45.	d	(drink)	57.	k	(thanks)
34.	t	(faster)	46.	g	(glucose)	58.	d	(aphids)
35.	b	(table)	47.	b	(blanket)	59.	b	(shrubs)
36.	g	(aggravate)	48.	t	(strong)	60.	t	(mast)

C.   Written and Aural Presentation: Combined Positions

1.	t	9.	b	17.	k
2.	p	10.	d	18.	t
3.	k	11.	k	19.	b
4.	b	12.	g	20.	g
5.	t	13.	p	21.	p
6.	d	14.	g	22.	d
7.	g	15.	d	23.	t
8.	k	16.	p	24.	b

D.   Aural Only Presentation: Combined Positions

1.	b	(bereave)	10.	p	(limp)
2.	t	(lantern)	11.	g	(ghoulish)
3.	d	(frowned)	12.	b	(remember)
4.	k	(caravan)	13.	k	(queen)
5.	k	(maximum)	14.	t	(fraught)
6.	p	(pencil)	15.	g	(league)
7.	d	(weeding)	16.	p	(helpless)
8.	g	(frugal)	17.	d	(daring)
9.	t	(terrify)	18.	b	(blossom)

E.   Aural Only Presentation: Nonsense words

1.	p	(/æpos/)	7.	p	(/pwɪnə/)
2.	d	(/dɛʒɚn/)	8.	t	(/vutməf/)
3.	t	(/tevoz/)	9.	k	(/kæwənz/)
4.	b	(/bærəm/)	10.	g	(/ʒɚnug/)
5.	d	(/fwɑdiz/)	11.	g	(/ɑgwəve/)
6.	k	(/mikɪf/)	12.	b	(/ɛnbwɔə/)

F.   Sagittal Sections

1.	a	(jumble /b/)	7.	c	(flag /g/)
2.	b	(giant /t/)	8.	b	(Edith /d/)
3.	a	(lamprey /p/)	9.	a	(happen /p/)
4.	b	(staring /t/)	10.	c	(squeamish /k/)
5.	b	(medley /d/)	11.	c	(argue /g/)
6.	c	(canon /k/)	12.	a	(wobble /b/)

G. Final Exercise: Oral Stops

Real words

1.	p	t		(patron)	6.	b	k		(bicycle)
2.	t	t		(tantrum)	7.	d	b		(dribble)
3.	g	b		(gamble)	8.	b	k		(break)
4.	d	p	d	(dappled)	9.	k	d		(caldron)
5.	p	t	k	(lipstick)	10.	g	p		(grape)

Nonsense words

11.	b	d	k	(/bændek/)	15.	t	p	g	(/tɛpgæʃ/)
12.	g	b	t	(/gibət/)	16.	p	d	g	(/pʌdog/)
13.	d	k	p	(/dokəp/)	17.	k	b		(/kræsəb/)
14.	k	t	d	(/kutsəd/)					

NASAL STOP CONSONANTS

III. Self-Test

Real words

1.	n	m		(pneumatic)	6.	n	m		(bantam)
2.	ŋ	ŋ		(sinking)	7.	n	ŋ		(snowing)
3.	n	n		(banyan)	8.	n	m		(numbed)
4.	m	n		(manacle)	9.	ŋ			(blanket)
5.	n	n		(engine)	10.	n	m	ŋ	(naming)

Nonsense words

11.	m	n	(/moden/)
12.	n	ŋ	(/noŋk/)
13.	m	n	(/blæmplənt/)
14.	n	m	(/nimɪp/)
15.	n	m	(/gɪnrɪmp/)
16.	ŋ	m	(/dæŋtɵm/)
17.	m	ŋ	(/mɪblɔŋ/)
18.	n	ŋ	(/tinəŋk/)

IV.   Practice Exercise

A.   Yes-No Discriminations

	+	−			+	−	
1.	—	x	(/ɪgwu/)	7.	—	x	(/ɪdroʃ/)
2.	—	x	(/ɛrədɛg/)	8.	—	x	(/sligod/)
3.	x	—	(/swændo/)	9.	x	—	(/fwɔŋi/)
4.	x	—	(/ɪdlɔŋ/)	10.	—	x	(/bædlo/)
5.	x	—	(/æʒɑm/)	11.	x	—	(/zodɪm/)
6.	x	—	(/rɪmpe/)	12.	—	x	(/ifle/)

B.   Aural Only Presentation: Specific Positions

Initial position

1.	n	(gnash)	4.	n	(pneumatic)
2.	m	(macaroni)	5.	n	(nebulous)
3.	m	(magnify)	6.	m	(mandible)

Final position

7.	m	(bedlam)	12.	n	(reaction)
8.	n	(balloon)	13.	m	(lamb)
9.	ŋ	(fitting)	14.	ŋ	(wing)
10.	n	(barren)	15.	m	(groom)
11.	ŋ	(song)			

Medial position

16.	n	(Danish)	19.	m	(bumble)
17.	m	(damage)	20.	n	(conjecture)
18.	ŋ	(hanger)	21.	ŋ	(tangy)

Clusters

22.	m	(clamped)	26.	ŋ	(things)
23.	ŋ	(lynx)	27.	n	(snails)
24.	n	(hands)	28.	ŋ	(spanked)
25.	m	(smoky)			

C.   Written and Aural Presentation: Combined Positions

1.	n		6.	m
2.	ŋ		7.	n
3.	m		8.	m
4.	n		9.	ŋ
5.	ŋ			

D. *Aural Only Presentation: Combined Positions—Real Words*

1.	n	(fringe)	4.	ŋ	(anger)
2.	m	(timber)	5.	ŋ	(songs)
3.	n	(knock)	6.	m	(lamps)

E. *Aural Only Presentation: Combined Positions—Nonsense Words*

1.	ŋ	(/dərɛŋi/)	4.	m	(/ɪlmodi/)
2.	n	(/ginro/)	5.	n	(/bɛgrɪn/)
3.	ŋ	(/ʃilfɪŋ/)	6.	m	(/smolɪk/)

F. **Sagittal Sections**

1.	c	(bring /ŋ/)	4.	c	(linger /ŋ/)
2.	a	(familiar /m/)	5.	b	(errant /n/)
3.	b	(bandage /n/)	6.	a	(timber /m/)

G. **Final Exercise: Nasal Stops**

Real words

1.	m	n		(mangy)	5.	ŋ		(brink)
2.	m	n	n	(imagination)	6.	n	ŋ	(snapping)
3.	ŋ			(anchor)	7.	m		(brooms)
4.	m			(carom)	8.	m	n	(moons)

Nonsense words

9.	n	m	(/ɛndəm/)	12.	m	ŋ	(/smæŋk/)
10.	m	n	(/mærən/)	13.	ŋ		(/ʃɪŋɪs/)
11.	n	ŋ	(/nɛskɪŋ/)	14.	n	m	(/snimɪt/)

Answers: Laboratory Session 2
Fricatives and Affricates

SELF-TEST: FRICATIVES AND AFFRICATES

Real words

1.	s	tʃ		(searching)	8.	v	f	ʃ	(verification)
2.	v	s		(marvelous)	9.	s	ʃ		(squash)
3.	f	s		(fantastic)	10.	ʃ	f		(sheriff)
4.	dʒ	dʒ		(judging)	11.	θ	s		(toothpaste)
5.	v	ʒ		(television)	12.	z	z		(zeros)
6.	f	θ		(philanthropy)	13.	ð	z		(wreaths)
7.	θ	f		(thoroughfare)	14.	ð	z		(those)
					15.	tʃ	s		(chase)

Nonsense words

16.	ʃ	v	z	(/ʃovəz/)	21.	θ	s	tʃ	(/θæsotʃ/)
17.	ð	f	s	(/ðɛmfɪs/)	22.	z	ʃ	ʒ	(/zoʃɪʒ/)
18.	v	dʒ	θ	(/vodʒəθ/)	23.	tʃ	h		(/tʃænho/)
19.	s	ʒ	f	(/sɛʒæf/)	24.	s	v		(/splɪndov/)
20.	f	θ	ʃ	(/fuθɪʃ/)	25.	h	ð	dʒ	(/hæðədʒ/)

PRACTICE EXERCISES

A.   Yes-No Discriminations

Fricatives

	+	−			+	−	
1.	x	—	(lather)	6.	—	x	(remain)
2.	x	—	(calf)	7.	—	x	(woman)
3.	—	x	(ladder)	8.	x	—	(buzzing)
4.	x	—	(thing)	9.	—	x	(errant)
5.	x	—	(ceremony)	10.	—	x	(temper)

Affricates

	+	−			+	−	
11.	x	—	(hatching)	14.	x	—	(energy)
12.	—	x	(vase)	15.	—	x	(fifth)
13.	x	—	(watch)	16.	—	x	(glasses)

Voiced Fricatives or Voiced Affricates

	+	−			+	−	
17.	—	x	(sentry)	21.	—	x	(hamper)
18.	x	—	(venture)	22.	—	x	(fox)
19.	—	x	(thin)	23.	x	—	(brother)
20.	x	—	(garage)	24.	x	—	(nosy)

Sibilants

	+	−			+	−	
25.	x	—	(dance)	30.	x	—	(latch)
26.	x	—	(wash)	31.	x	—	(budge)
27.	—	x	(heaven)	32.	—	x	(although)
28.	—	x	(wealth)	33.	—	x	(raft)
29.	x	—	(rosy)	34.	—	x	(wreath)

B.   *Written and Aural Presentation: Specific Positions*

Initial position

1. s
2. tʃ
3. f
4. θ
5. v
6. ð
7. z
8. dʒ
9. h
10. ʃ

Final position

11. dʒ
12. θ
13. v
14. ʃ
15. s
16. ð
17. f
18. ʒ
19. z
20. tʃ

Medial position

21. θ
22. tʃ
23. f
24. ʒ
25. v
26. dʒ
27. ʃ
28. s
29. z
30. ð

Clusters

31. θ
32. ʃ
33. f
34. s
35. s
36. dʒ
37. z
38. θ
39. ð
40. tʃ
41. f
42. ʃ
43. v
44. ʒ

C. Aural Only Presentation: Specific Positions

Initial position

1.	tʃ	(chowder)
2.	θ	(think)
3.	f	(phonograph)
4.	s	(simple)
5.	ð	(there)
6.	ʃ	(champagne)
7.	h	(hemp)
8.	v	(vampire)
9.	dʒ	(jingle)
10.	z	(zodiac)

Final position

11.	θ	(birth)
12.	f	(calf)
13.	dʒ	(badge)
14.	s	(caboose)
15.	tʃ	(reach)
16.	ʃ	(lush)
17.	v	(alcove)
18.	z	(pose)
19.	ð	(loathe)
20.	ʒ	(loge)

Medial position

21.	θ	(frothy)
22.	z	(Susan)
23.	ʃ	(fashion)
24.	f	(careful)
25.	dʒ	(angel)
26.	v	(seventy)
27.	ʒ	(treasure)
28.	tʃ	(bachelor)
29.	ð	(hither)
30.	s	(parsley)

Clusters

31.	θ	(thrill)
32.	s	(split)
33.	f	(flame)
34.	ʃ	(shrine)
35.	dʒ	(hinge)
36.	θ	(wealth)
37.	s	(fence)
38.	ʃ	(wished)
39.	v	(carve)
40.	z	(beds)
41.	f	(laughed)
42.	tʃ	(lynch)

D. Written and Aural Presentation: Combined Positions

1.	ʃ			13.	v	ʒ
2.	z			14.	dʒ	z
3.	z			15.	θ	f
4.	θ			16.	s	dʒ
5.	ð			17.	h	ð
6.	f			18.	f	tʃ
7.	ʃ			19.	s	s
8.	tʃ			20.	z	θ
9.	θ	s	s	21.	v	ʒ
10.	tʃ	dʒ		22.	f	f
11.	v	z		23.	ʃ	z
12.	ʃ	f		24.	h	z

E. Aural Only Presentation: Combined Positions—Real Words

1.	s		(nasty)
2.	θ		(bathtub)
3.	tʃ		(ketchup)
4.	dʒ		(merger)
5.	z		(ozone)
6.	ʃ		(lash)
7.	θ	s	(toothpaste)
8.	s	ð	(seething)
9.	ʃ	s	(luscious)

10.	ʃ	v		(shrivel)
11.	v	s		(verse)
12.	s	ð		(soothed)
13.	ʒ	z		(measures)
14.	dʒ	z	f	(Joseph)
15.	h	tʃ		(hitch)
16.	f	θ		(filth)
17.	s	dʒ		(strange)
18.	tʃ	s	z	(chancellors)

F. Aural Only Presentation: Combined Positions—Nonsense Words

1.	h			(/ɛnhot/)
2.	θ			(/θrɪmrəp/)
3.	s			(/dɪsnok/)
4.	ʒ			(/bəluʒ/)
5.	h	θ		(/hɛθdəm/)
6.	s	v	z	(/stɪnvoz/)
7.	tʃ	ʃ	f	(/tʃʌmʃɛf/)

8.	z	ʒ	θ	(/zoʒɛθ/)
9.	v	ð		(/vɛmað/)
10.	f	ð	s	(/fɪðɚs/)
11.	ð	ʃ		(/ðɪnɪʃ/)
12.	dʒ	tʃ		(/dʒɛmtʃo/)
13.	ʃ	dʒ		(/ʃrɛmɛndʒ/)
14.	f	z	tʃ	(/frɪzlotʃ/)

G. Sagittal Sections

1.	b	(phlegmatic /f/)
2.	a	(tithe /ð/)
3.	c	(cent /s/)
4.	a	(throw /θ/)

5.	b	(covert /v/)
6.	d	(azure /ʒ/)
7.	d	(chalet /ʃ/)
8.	c	(cousin /z/)

H. Final Exercise: Aural Only Presentation—Combined Positions

Real words

1.	ʒ			(garage)
2.	s	z		(season)
3.	θ	ʃ		(threshing)
4.	dʒ	s	f	(justify)
5.	s	dʒ		(sage)
6.	z	f		(zephyr)
7.	f	dʒ		(fledgling)
8.	ð	z		(those)

9.	θ	s		(thirsty)
10.	f	ð		(father)
11.	ʃ	ð		(sheathe)
12.	tʃ	dʒ		(challenger)
13.	f	v	ʃ	(feverish)
14.	s	θ	s	(stealthiness)
15.	v	ʒ	z	(visions)

Nonsense words

16.	θ	z		(/θɪnzot/)
17.	ʒ	ð		(/ʒaɪðɛŋ/)
18.	f	s		(/flɛtos/)
19.	ð	ʒ		(/ðæmɪʒ/)
20.	v	dʒ		(/vɔɪmadʒ/)

21.	θ	ʒ		(/bɪəreʒ/)
22.	ð	ð		(/ðɪmnæð/)
23.	f	θ		(/fonuθ/)
24.	dʒ	v	ʒ	(/dʒævɪʒ/)
25.	f	z	dʒ	(/frɪzlodʒ/)

Answers: Laboratory Session 3
Liquids and Glides

III. Self-Test

Real words

1.	l	j		(bullion)	6.	r	w		(carwash)
2.	w	r		(thwart)	7.	r	w		(wristwatch)
3.	j	l		(bucolic)	8.	j	l		(yelling)
4.	l	r		(glare)	9.	ʍ	l		(wheel)
5.	r	l	r	(forlorn)	10.	ʍ	r	r	(wherefore)

Nonsense words

11.	l	r		(/læmbro/)	15.	ʍ	l	r	(/ʍɪlpɑr/)
12.	j	r		(/jorɪŋ/)	16.	r	j		(/rofjæm/)
13.	w	l	r	(/wɪnglɑr/)	17.	j	ʍ	l	(/jɛtʍɛl/)
14.	l	j	r	(/sɪljor/)	18.	l	w		(/lægwæm/)

IV.   Practice Exercises

A.   Yes-No Discriminations

Liquids

	+	−			+	−	
1.	x	—	(television)	5.	x	—	(belt)
2.	—	x	(vanish)	6.	x	—	(wrung)
3.	—	x	(basin)	7.	—	x	(squash)
4.	x	—	(worn)	8.	—	x	(coast)

Lateral liquids

	+	−			+	−	
9.	x	—	(coalition)	12.	x	—	(pleasure)
10.	—	x	(beverage)	13.	x	—	(following)
11.	—	x	(ambitious)	14.	—	x	(arrogant)

Glides

	+	−			+	−	
15.	x	—	(quite)	19.	x	—	(billion)
16.	—	x	(manager)	20.	x	—	(languish)
17.	x	—	(accuse)	21.	—	x	(crumbly)
18.	—	x	(clash)	22.	—	x	(enjoy)

Labial-velar glides

	+	−			+	−	
23.	—	x	(useful)	26.	x	—	(sanguine)
24.	x	—	(switch)	27	—	x	(energetic)
25.	—	x	(heavy)	28.	x	—	(one)

B. Aural Only Presentation: Specific Positions

Initial Position			*Medial Position*		
1.	ʍ	(whine)	15.	w	(seaweed)
2.	j	(unity)	16.	l	(elbow)
3.	r	(wrought)	17.	ʍ	(nowhere)
4.	l	(listen)	18.	j	(vacuum)
5.	w	(wine)	19.	w	(unwind)
6.	j	(young)	20.	l	(falling)
7.	r	(wrinkle)	21.	ʍ	(somewhat)
8.	w	(one)	22.	r	(orange)
9.	l	(limpid)	23.	j	(beyond)
10.	ʍ	(whimper)	24.	r	(tomorrow)

Final Position			*Clusters*					
11.	l	(school)	25.	w	(sway)	30.	r	(prince)
12.	r	(feldspar)	26.	j	(fury)	31.	w	(Dwayne)
13.	r	(chair)	27.	w	(dwelling)	32.	r	(barn)
14.	l	(parole)	28.	w	(twig)	33.	j	(cute)
			29.	l	(held)	34.	l	(split)

C. Written and Aural Presentation: Combined Positions

No.				No.			
1.	l			11.	ʍ	l	r
2.	w			12.	l	j	
3.	j			13.	w	l	
4.	w			14.	ʍ	r	
5.	r			15.	j	r	r
6.	w	l		16.	w	r	
7.	j	l		17.	r	w	
8.	l	w		18.	j	l	
9.	r	r		19.	l	r	
10.	w	r		20.	ʍ	l	

D. Aural Only Presentation: Combined Positions—Real Words

1. r		(wreck)	11. j j		(union)
2. ʍ		(whiff)	12. r l		(revolve)
3. l		(melody)	13. w l r		(wallboard)
4. j		(banyan)	14. j l		(yellow)
5. w		(anguish)	15. l l		(legal)
6. l j		(stallion)	16. ʍ r w l		(whippoorwill)
7. w r		(wearing)	17. l r		(already)
8. l r		(lamprey)	18. r r		(armchair)
9. r r l		(rhetorical)	19. j r		(furious)
10. w l		(quietly)	20. l l		(flawless)

E. Aural Only Presentation: Combined Positions—Nonsense Words

1. ʍ	(/ʍɪnt/)	8. j w	(/jæbwən/)
2. l	(/splʌndɪʃ/)	9. l ʍ r	(/lʌmʍɑr/)
3. r	(/stɔrf/)	10. w w	(/wɛmtwɪf/)
4. w	(/gwɛsdɪm/)	11. r l	(/bufrol/)
5. j	(/fjuməʒ/)	12. l r	(/klæro/)
6. l r	(/lɑrɪŋ/)	13. j r	(pjudmɪr/)
7. r l j	(/rɔljən/)	14. r l j	(/rɪljop/)

F. Sagittal Sections

1. b	(corps /r/)	6. a	(fellow /l/)
2. d	(twenty /w/)	7. c	(yawn /j/)
3. a	(link /l/)	8. d	(wagon /w/)
4. b	(write /r/)	9. d	(whim /ʍ/)
5. d	(watch /w/)	10. c	(feud /j/)

Answers: Laboratory Review I
English Consonants

PRACTICE EXERCISE

Real words

1.	h	r	t	ɵ	r	b	(heartthrob)
2.	p	r	v	s			(privacy)
3.	v	k	j	ʃ	n		(evacuation)
4.	l	b	r	t	r		(laboratory)
5.	dʒ	k	r	b	t		(jack rabbit)
6.	m	s	tʃ	f			(mischief)
7.	n	v	ʒ	n			(invasion)
8.	k	r	dʒ	l			(cordially)
9.	g	l	s	n	d		(glistened)
10.	b	ɵ	t	b			(bathtub)

11.	ʍ	p	r	w	l		(whippoorwill)
12.	z	p	ŋ				(zipping)
13.	d	m	dʒ	z			(damages)
14.	ʃ	m	n	ʃ	p		(showmanship)
15.	ð	r	b	t	s		(thereabouts)
16.	r	ð	ŋ				(writhing)
17.	j	ɵ	f	l			(youthful)
18.	l	ŋ	g	w	dʒ		(language)
19.	v	k	r	s			(vicarious)
20.	f	s	n	t	ŋ		(fascinating)

Nonsense words

21.	g	ð	m			(/gʌðəm/)
22.	h	z	g			(/hɛzɪg/)
23.	p	ð	r	v	tʃ	(/pʌðərævɪtʃ/)
24.	ʍ	n	ʒ	d		(/ʍʌnʒaɪd/)
25.	n	m	ŋ	ɵ		(/næmɪŋeɵ/)

26.	ð	m	b	l	k	(/ðʌmbələk/)
27.	t	n	ɵ	ʃ		(/tɛneɵʃ/)
28.	h	w	ʃ	s	l	ŋ	(/hɛweʃəslɪŋ/)
29.	f	w	m	j	t	(/fwɪmjɛt/)
30.	s	ð	l	ʒ		(/sɛðələʒ/)

Answers: Laboratory Session 4
Front and Back Vowels

III. Self-Test: Front and Back Vowels

Real words

1. u ⍵   (spoonful)
2. ɔ ɪ   (awning)
3. i o   (keynote)
4. e ɔ   (baseball)
5. i u ɪ   (regrouping)
6. ɛ ɪ e   (hesitate)

7. æ o ɛ   (arrowhead)
8. u æ ɪ   (pneumatic)
9. æ ɑ ɪ   (halfhearted)
10. ɪ æ ɪ ɪ   (establishing)
11. ɛ i æ ɪ   (geriatrics)
12. i æ ɪ i   (reality)

Nonsense words

13. ɔ æ   (/kɔwæp/)
14. ɑ ⍵   (/zɑlfⓈs/)
15. ɔ ⍵   (/sɔbⓈt/)
16. ɑ u   (/gɑlut/)

17. i æ ɪ   (/vikælɪp/)
18. i o e   (/finotet/)
19. ɛ u e ɑ   (/dɛmustenɑt/)
20. æ o ɪ i   (/bælosɪfit/)

IV. Practice Exercises

A.   Yes-No Discriminations

Front vowels

	+	–			+	–	
1.	—	x	(owner)	6.	—	x	(football)
2.	—	x	(fruit)	7.	—	x	(paw)
3.	x	—	(ember)	8.	x	—	(Easter)
4.	x	—	(king)	9.	—	x	(stop)
5.	x	—	(aloe)	10.	x	—	(waist)

Back vowels

	+	–			+	–	
11.	x	—	(soap)	16.	—	x	(handy)
12.	x	—	(loot)	17.	—	x	(seam)
13.	—	x	(enter)	18.	x	—	(shawl)
14.	x	—	(soot)	19.	—	x	(haste)
15.	—	x	(sing)	20.	x	—	(soft)

B. Written and Aural Presentation: Combined Positions—Subclasses of Vowels

Front vowels

1.	e		8.	ı	
2.	ı		9.	i	
3.	i		10.	ε	
4.	æ		11.	æ	ı
5.	e		12.	ı	e
6.	ε		13.	ε	ı
7.	æ		14.	ı	ε

Back vowels

15.	o		22.	ɔ	
16.	u		23.	o	
17.	ɔ		24.	ꭢ	
18.	ꭢ		25.	o	o
19.	ɑ		26.	ɔ	o
20.	u		27.	o	ꭢ
21.	ɑ		28.	ɑ	o

C.   Aural Only Presentation: Specific Positions

Initial position

1.	e	(ache)	6.	ı	(ingest)
2.	æ	(ask)	7.	ɔ	(all)
3.	i	(east)	8.	ɛ	(enter)
4.	ɑ	(art)	9.	o	(oak)
5.	u	(oodles)	10.	ɑ	(almond)

Medial position

11.	u	(fool)	16.	e	(fate)
12.	ᴜ	(hook)	17.	ɔ	(caught)
13.	ɑ	(psalm)	18.	ɛ	(fence)
14.	ı	(thing)	19.	æ	(past)
15.	o	(hope)	20.	i	(feast)

Final position

21.	ɔ	(thaw)	24.	e	(lamprey)
22.	o	(auto)	25.	u	(threw)
23.	i	(kitty)	26.	i	(free)

D.   Written and Aural Presentation: Combined Positions

1.	u		11.	ı	ᴜ	
2.	o		12.	u	ɔ	
3.	i		13.	ɛ	ı	
4.	ɔ		14.	u	ı	
5.	ı		15.	ɑ	u	
6.	ɛ		16.	ı	i	
7.	e		17.	u	æ	
8.	ᴜ		18.	ı	ɛ	ı
9.	æ		19.	æ	o	i
10.	ɑ		20.	ı	ı	i	e

E.   Aural Only Presentation: Combined Positions

1.	ʊ	(bush)	11.	ɑ	ɪ		(honest)
2.	ɔ	(fought)	12.	ɛ	o		(meadow)
3.	ɑ	(harp)	13.	o	e		(locate)
4.	ɛ	(spent)	14.	ɪ	ɛ		(insect)
5.	æ	(mash)	15.	u	ɪ		(cubic)
6.	ɪ	(stint)	16.	ʊ	i		(bushy)
7.	i	(least)	17.	ɪ	o	ɪ	(heroic)
8.	u	(loose)	18.	æ	ɪ	æ	(habitat)
9.	o	(coast)	19.	æ	o	ɪ	(aerobic)
10.	e	(bake)	20.	ɪ	æ	ɪ	i	(insanity)

F.   Aural Only Presentation: Combined Positions—Nonsense Words

1.	ʊ	(/vʊst/)	11.	u	i		(/dulip/)
2.	ɪ	(/drɪnt/)	12.	ɑ	o		(/nɑbot/)
3.	æ	(/skræmp/)	13.	ɔ	ɪ		(/sɔmɪŋ/)
4.	ɔ	(/bɔlt/)	14.	ʊ	ɛ		(/stʊplɛk/)
5.	ɑ	(/dɑrst/)	15.	e	æ		(/petnæst/)
6.	i	(/grim/)	16.	u	i	o	(/juvinop/)
7.	u	(/wust/)	17.	ɔ	ɪ	ʊ	(/mɔsɪnʊk/)
8.	e	(/neks/)	18.	e	æ	i	(/letænti/)
9.	ɛ	(/flɛnt/)	19.	ɑ	ɛ	o	(/gɑrpɛdo/)
10.	o	(/trost/)	20.	æ	o	ɛ	i	(/mælosɛfit/)

Answers: Laboratory Session 5
Central Vowels and Diphthongs

III. Self-Test: Central vowels

Real words

1.	ʌ	ə		(button)	6.	ʌ	ɚ		(brother)
2.	ɝ	ə		(urban)	7.	ə	ʌ		(enough)
3.	ʌ	ɚ		(under)	8.	ʌ	ɚ	ʌ	(cummerbund)
4.	ɝ	ɚ		(further)	9.	ə	ʌ	ɚ	(another)
5.	ɝ	ə		(curtain)	10.	ʌ	ɚ	ə	(thunderous)

Nonsense words

11.	ɝ	ə		(/zɝnəp/)	15.	ʌ	ɚ	ʌ	(/ʌmɚsʌnd/)
12.	ʌ	ə		(/ kʌbəst/)	16.	ə	ɝ	ə	(/əzɝtlənd/)
13.	ə	ʌ	ə	(/ənʌstən/)	17.	ə	ɝ	ɚ	(/fənɝstɚ/)
14.	ə	ɝ	ɚ	(/bəlɝðɚ/)	18.	ə	ɝ	ə	ɚ	(/məlɝfdənɚ/)

CENTRAL VOWELS

IV. Practice Exercises

A. *Yes-No Discriminations*

Central vowels

	+	−			+	−	
1.	x	—	(enter)	5.	—	x	(only)
2.	x	—	(putty)	6.	x	—	(early)
3.	—	x	(side)	7.	x	—	(about)
4.	—	x	(hinge)	8.	—	x	(lace)

/ʌ/

	+	−			+	−	
9.	—	x	(pizza)	12.	—	x	(alone)
10.	x	—	(above)	13.	x	—	(blunt)
11.	x	—	(upper)	14.	—	x	(upon)

/ɝ/

	+	−			+	−	
15.	x	—	(inert)	18.	x	—	(burning)
16.	—	x	(errand)	19.	—	x	(teacher)
17.	—	x	(bazaar)	20.	x	—	(furnish)

/ə/

	+	−			+	−	
21.	x	—	(among)	23.	x	—	(moment)
22.	—	x	(butcher)	24.	—	x	(fussy)

/ɚ/

	+	−			+	−	
25.	x	—	(brother)	27.	—	x	(thirsty)
26.	x	—	(pertain)	28.	—	x	(earnest)

B.   Aural Only Presentation: Specific Positions

Initial position

1.	ʌ	(utter)	4.	ɚ	(urbane)
2.	ɝ	(early)	5.	ʌ	(ultimate)
3.	ə	(atone)	6.	ə	(among)

Medial position

7.	ɝ	(inert)	10.	ɚ	(survive)
8.	ʌ	(lucky)	11.	ɝ	(learn)
9.	ə	(debris)	12.	ɚ	(pertain)

Final position

13.	ə	(banana)	16.	ɚ	(injure)
14.	ɚ	(bother)	17.	ɝ	(deter)
15.	ɝ	(recur)	18.	ə	(sofa)

C.   Written and Aural Presentation: Combined Positions

1.	ʌ			6.	ɝ	ʌ	
2.	ɝ			7.	ə	ʌ	
3.	ʌ	ɚ		8.	ɝ	ɚ	ə
4.	ə	ʌ		9.	ʌ	ɚ	ʌ
5.	ɝ	ɚ		10.	ə	ʌ	ɚ

D.   Aural Only Presentation: Combined Positions

1.	ʌ			(dust)	6.	ɝ	ɚ			(burner)
2.	ɝ			(mirth)	7.	ʌ	ɚ			(stubborn)
3.	ə	ʌ		(among)	8.	ɝ	ɚ	ɚ		(murderer)
4.	ə	ɝ		(submerged)	9.	ʌ	ɚ	ʌ		(blunderbuss)
5.	ɝ	ə		(irksome)	10.	ʌ	ɚ	ʌ	ɚ	(undercover)

E.   Aural Only Presentation: Combined Positions—Nonsense Words

1.	ʌ			(/slʌb/)
2.	ɝ			(/dɝlz/)
3.	ʌ	ɚ		(/tʃʌnɚt/)
4.	ɝ	ɚ		(/vɝdɚk/)
5.	ɝ	ə		(/bɝlə/)

6.	ʌ	ɚ	ʌ		(/mʌndɚdʌsk/)
7.	ɝ	ə	ɚ		(/fɝbələɝʒ/)
8.	ə	ɝ	ə		(/tənɝʃən/)
9.	ɝ	ə	ə		(/ɝbəsə/)
10.	ʌ	ə	ʌ	ɚ	(/sʌndəgʌlɚ/)

F.   Final Exercise: Central Vowels

Real words

1.	ɝ		(hurt)
2.	ʌ		(cut)
3.	ɝ		(flirt)
4.	ʌ		(such)
5.	ʌ	ɚ	(supper)
6.	ʌ	ə	(husband)
7.	ɚ	ɝ	(perverse)

8.	ɝ	ɚ		(murder)
9.	ɝ	ə		(urban)
10.	ʌ	ə		(oven)
11.	ɝ	ə		(bourbon)
12.	ə	ʌ	ə	(combustion)
13.	ʌ	ɚ	ɝ	(thunderbird)
14.	ʌ	ɚ	ə	(cumbersome)

Nonsense words

15.	ɝ	ɚ		(/dɝðɚ/)
16.	ə	ʌ		(/məθʌŋ/)
17.	ə	ʌ	ɚ	(/əpʌmɚ/)

18.	ɝ	ə	ə	(/gɝdʒələ/)
19.	ə	ɝ	ə	(/lətʃɝməl/)
20.	ʌ	ɚ	ʌ	ɚ	(/ʌmɚdʌvɚ/)

III. Self-Test: Diphthongs

Real words

1.	ɔɪ		(Joyce)
2.	o		(ago)
3.	aɪ		(blind)
4.	aʊ		(around)
5.	eɪ		(maze)
6.	aɪ		(deny)
7.	aʊ		(county)
8.	eɪ		(grazing)

9.	ɔɪ		(toiling)
10.	oʊ		(unknown)
11.	eɪ	aʊ	(playground)
12.	aʊ	aɪ	(outright)
13.	eɪ		(layout)
14.	aɪ	aʊ	(nightgown)
15.	aɪ	aʊ	(icehouse)

Nonsense words

16.	aʊ	aɪ		(/aʊklaɪə/)
17.	ɔɪ	aʊ		(/gɔɪstaʊ/)
18.	aɪ	oʊ		(/aɪnsoʊz/)
19.	aʊ	ɔɪ		(/ʃaʊkɔɪm/)
20.	oʊ	aɪ		(/oʊmzaɪ/)

21.	eɪ	aʊ		(/reɪnkaʊn/)
22.	ɔɪ	aɪ		(/ɔɪblaɪ/)
23.	aʊ	eɪ		(/dʒaʊsreɪz/)
24.	ɔɪ	aʊ		(/bɔɪzdaʊnd/)
25.	oʊ	eɪ		(/spoʊngeɪv/)

IV. Practice Exercises

A.   *Yes-No Discriminations*

Diphthongs

	+	−			+	−	
1.	x	—	(noisy)	6.	x	—	(today)
2.	x	—	(mountain)	7.	—	x	(thirsty)
3.	—	x	(flute)	8.	—	x	(booklet)
4.	—	x	(beast)	9.	—	x	(combustion)
5.	x	—	(homely)	10.	x	—	(might)

/aɪ/

	+	−			+	−	
11.	—	x	(same)	14.	x	—	(invite)
12.	x	—	(lime)	15.	x	—	(aisle)
13.	—	x	(useful)	16.	—	x	(liter)

/aʊ/

	+	−			+	−	
17.	x	—	(town)	20.	—	x	(loiter)
18.	—	x	(seize)	21.	—	x	(ace)
19.	x	—	(fountain)	22.	x	—	(abound)

/ɔɪ/

	+	−			+	−	
23.	x	—	(thyroid)	26.	x	—	(loiter)
24.	—	x	(louder)	27.	x	—	(hoisting)
25.	—	x	(vein)	28.	—	x	(wine)

B.   Aural Only Presentation: Specific Positions

Initial position

1.	aɪ	(item)	6.	aɪ	(ivy)
2.	aʊ	(ours)	7.	oʊ	(over)
3.	ɔɪ	(oink)	8.	aʊ	(ouch)
4.	oʊ	(omen)	9.	eɪ	(able)
5.	eɪ	(age)	10.	ɔɪ	(oiler)

Medial position

11.	ɔɪ	(moist)	16.	oʊ	(nose)
12.	aɪ	(might)	17.	eɪ	(label)
13.	oʊ	(roan)	18.	aɪ	(rise)
14.	aʊ	(bounce)	19.	ɔɪ	(join)
15.	eɪ	(veil)	20.	aʊ	(growl)

Final position

21.	aʊ	(brow)	26.	eɪ	(display)
22.	aɪ	(try)	27.	oʊ	(forgo)
23.	ɔɪ	(destroy)	28.	aʊ	(vow)
24.	oʊ	(low)	29.	ɔɪ	(deploy)
25.	aɪ	(sigh)	30.	eɪ	(say)

C.   Written and Aural Presentation: Combined Positions

1.	oʊ		9.	ɔɪ	
2.	aʊ		10.	aʊ	
3.	aɪ		11.	aʊ	aɪ
4.	eɪ		12.	aɪ	aɪ
5.	ɔɪ		13.	aʊ	ɔɪ
6.	aɪ		14.	eɪ	aɪ
7.	eɪ		15.	aʊ	aʊ
8.	oʊ				

D. Aural Only Presentation: Combined Positions

1.	oʊ		(moan)	9.	eɪ	(remain)
2.	ɔɪ		(destroy)	10.	oʊ eɪ	(obey)
3.	aʊ		(couch)	11.	eɪ eɪ	(payday)
4.	aɪ		(mice)	12.	aɪ aʊ	(nightowl)
5.	ɔɪ		(goiter)	13.	ɔɪ aʊ	(boy scout)
6.	oʊ		(hello)	14.	aɪ aʊ	(lighthouse)
7.	aɪ		(icon)	15.	eɪ aɪ	(daylight)
8.	aʊ		(ouster)			

E. Aural Only Presentation: Combined Positions—Nonsense Words

1.	ɔɪ aʊ	(/ɔɪdraʊ/)	6.	eɪ oʊ	(/eɪmloʊv/)
2.	oʊ aɪ	(/oʊzaɪt/)	7.	ɔɪ aʊ	(/zɔɪmaʊnɪŋ/)
3.	ɔɪ aɪ	(/fɔɪdlaɪz/)	8.	aʊ ɔɪ	(/baʊldɔɪt/)
4.	aʊ aɪ	(/aʊdraɪf/)	9.	eɪ aʊ	(/geɪnʃaʊ/)
5.	aʊ eɪ	(/daʊbeɪn/)	10.	oʊ aɪ	(/tʃoʊdʒaɪ/)

F. Final Exercise: Diphthongs

Real words

1.	eɪ		(lazy)	9.	ɔɪ	(convoy)
2.	aɪ		(assignment)	10.	aʊ	(frown)
3.	ɔɪ		(cloister)	11.	aʊ aʊ	(downtown)
4.	aʊ		(bountiful)	12.	eɪ aɪ	(daytime)
5.	eɪ		(mailman)	13.	aɪ aʊ	(eyebrow)
6.	oʊ		(boulder)	14.	oʊ aʊ	(snowplow)
7.	aɪ		(lighter)	15.	aɪ ɔɪ	(thyroid)
8.	oʊ		(alone)			

Nonsense words

16.	aʊ aɪ	(/haʊmaɪt/)	19.	ɔɪ oʊ	(/ɔɪstoʊ/)
17.	aɪ oʊ	(/saɪtboʊ/)	20.	aʊ aɪ	(/braʊdaɪt/)
18.	eɪ aʊ	(/neɪzaʊp/)	21.	ɔɪ eɪ	(/fɔɪbeɪʒ/)

COMBINED EXERCISE: CENTRAL VOWELS AND DIPHTHONGS

Real words

1.	ʌ	ɚ		(mother)	8.	aɪ	ɔɪ		(highboy)
2.	ə	oʊ		(atoned)	9.	ɝ	aʊ		(birdhouse)
3.	eɪ	eɪ		(heyday)	10.	ɔɪ	ɚ	ə	(boisterous)
4.	aʊ	ə		(mountain)	11.	ʌ	ɚ	aʊ	(thundercloud)
5.	eɪ	aɪ		(daytime)	12.	ʌ	ɚ	ɝ	(undershirt)
6.	oʊ	ɚ		(loner)	13.	ə	aɪ	ə	(asylum)
7.	ʌ	ɝ		(sunburst)	14.	ɝ	ə	aɪ	(burglarize)

Nonsense words

15.	ɔɪ	aɪ		(/fɔɪtaɪ/)	19.	ɔɪ	ɝ	ə		(/pɔɪnɝʒən/)
16.	ɝ	aʊ		(/gɝlaʊv/)	20.	ɝ	eɪ	ə		(/bɝneɪəs/)
17.	ʌ	oʊ		(/mʌstoʊz/)	21.	aɪ	ʌ	ə		(/naɪlʌstək/)
18.	eɪ	oʊ		(/dʒeɪmoʊ/)	22.	ʌ	ə	aʊ	ɚ	(/sʌndəbaʊdɚ/)

Answers: Laboratory Review II
Consonants, Vowels, and Diphthongs

PRACTICE EXERCISE A: VOWELS AND DIPHTHONGS

Real words

1.	i	i	(beastly)		14.	ɝ	ɔɪ				(turquoise)
2.	æ	ɚ	(after)		15.	aʊ	aɪ				(cowhide)
3.	ɔ	ɪ	(fawning)		16.	ə	aɪ				(maligned)
4.	ɔɪ	ɪ	(voyage)		17.	ɝ	ɪ	ɚ			(furniture)
5.	ɝ	i	(thirsty)		18.	æ	ɑ	ɪ			(admonish)
6.	aɪ	i	(ice cream)		19.	ə	ɪ	ɚ			(familiar)
7.	aʊ	ɚ	(flounder)		20.	ʌ	ɚ	ʊ			(understood)
8.	ʌ	ɚ	(brother)		21.	o	e	ə			(donation)
9.	ɛ	ɪ	(getting)		22.	ə	u	ə			(allusion)
10.	ə	eɪ	(parade)		23.	ʊ	ɪ	ə			(fulfillment)
11.	u	ɛ	(bootleg)		24.	ə	æ	ə	i		(analogy)
12.	ə	oʊ	(abode)		25.	ʌ	ɚ	aɪ			(summertime)
13.	ɔ	ə	(lawful)		26.	ɪ	ɛ	ə	e	ə	(investigation)

Nonsense words

27.	u	ɑ	i	(/fulɑni/)		32.	ɔ	ʊ	i	(/kɔbʊtsi/)
28.	ɔɪ	ɚ		(/zɔɪstɚ/)		33.	ɪ	oʊ		(/fɪstoʊ/)
29.	ɝ	aʊ		(/bɝmaʊʒ/)		34.	o	æ	ɔɪ	(/sonæstɔɪ/)
30.	aɪ	ʌ	ə	(/faɪlʌstəs/)		35.	ɪ	ə	ɪ	(/mɪlədʒɪnts/)
31.	ɑ	u	eɪ	(/mɑluneɪ/)		36.	ɛ	æ	ə	ə	(/ɛmbæʃənə/)

PRACTICE EXERCISE B: CONSONANTS, VOWELS, AND DIPHTHONGS

Real words

1. / g   l   æ   s   ɪ   z /   (glasses)
2. / j   u   θ   f   ə   l /   (youthful)
3. / tʃ   ɔ   k   l   ɪ   t /   (chocolate)
4. / w   ɝ   θ   ʍ   aɪ   l /   (worthwhile)
5. / f   ɑ   r   m   ə   s   i /   (pharmacy)
6. / ɛ   n   dʒ   ɔɪ   m   ə   n   t /   (enjoyment)
7. / ɪ   n   ɛ   v   ɪ   t   ə   b   l   i /   (inevitably)
8. /raɪðɪŋ/   (writhing)
9. /hæpinɛs/   (happiness)
10. /dʒaɪgæntɪk/   (gigantic)
11. /dɪkʃənɛri/   (dictionary)

Nonsense words

12. / z   ʌ   p   ɚ   z /
13. / eɪ   n   b   oʊ   ʒ /
14. / s   n   e   s   t   o   p /
15. / ʃɔmtʃa /
16. /dɛfjuts/

Answers: Laboratory Session 6
Diacritics

III.   Self-Test

Real words

1.	[sĩŋkʰ]	(sink)	6.	[s̪wɛɫ]	(swell)
2.	[k̪ʰuɫ]	(cool)	7.	[əbaɔt˺]	(about)
3.	[bɝ˖dn̩]	(burden)	8.	[mɪs̪ɫ]	(missile)
4.	[nãɪ̃n̪θ]	(ninth)	9.	[pʰʊɫd̪]	(pulled)
5.	[ɛgz̪]	(eggs)	10.	[sk̪ ꞊ upʰ]	(scoop)

Nonsense words

11.	[blæ̃ntʰ]	14.	[dʒɛs̪l̩]
12.	[t̪ʰwɪpʰ]	15.	[əsk̪ ꞊ ĩŋkʰ]
13.	[sɪpɪg̪]	16.	[pʰʌdn̩]

IV.   Practice Exercises

A.   *Yes-No Discriminations*

Aspirated stops

	+	−			+	−	
1.	x	—	(ask)	4.	x	—	(telling)
2.	—	x	(spin)	5.	x	—	(pencil)
3.	—	x	(action)	6.	—	x	(star)

Nasalized vowels

	+	−			+	−	
7.	x	—	(pin)	10.	x	—	(can)
8.	—	x	(ask)	11.	—	x	(heroic)
9.	—	x	(fate)	12.	x	—	(ounce)

Velarized /l/

	+	−			+	−	
13.	x	—	(sold)	16.	—	x	(limb)
14.	—	x	(last)	17.	x	—	(hole)
15.	x	—	(petal)	18.	—	x	(sling)

B.   Written and Aural Presentation: Specific Positions

Initial position

1.   æ̃

2.   kʰ

3.   tʰ

4.   ɛ̃

5.   pʰ

6.   k̫ʰ

Medial position

7.   t˭

8.   pʰ

9.   æ̃

10.   ł

11.   k̫ʰ

12.   ɛ̃

Final position

13.   tˀ

14.   ł

15.   n̩

16.   kʰ

17.   ł̩

18.   ʐ̥

Clusters

19.   p˭

20.   ł

21.   k̫˭

22.   k̫ʰ

23.   ł

24.   k̫ʰ

C.   Aural Only Presentation: Specific Positions

Initial position					Final position			
1.	s̪ʷ		(suit)		13.	t̚		(flat)
2.	pʰ		(pitch)		14.	ŋ̩		(kitten)
3.	æ̃		(ant)		15.	ɫ		(pole)
4.	t̪ʰʷ	(2)	(tune)		16.	pʰ		(sip)
5.	kʰ		(king)		17.	g̥		(fog)
6.	æ̃		(anxious)		18.	ɫ̩	(2)	(whistle)

Medial position					Clusters			
7.	t̪ʰʷ	(2)	(atone)		19.	tʰ		(mist)
8.	ɫ		(bowling)		20.	p˭		(spill)
9.	t̪˭ʷ	(2)	(astute)		21.	kʰʷ	(2)	(quick)
10.	æ̃		(dance)		22.	t̪˭ʷ	(2)	(stool)
11.	pʰ		(applause)		23.	s̪ʷ		(swing)
12.	k˭		(ascribe)		24.	k˭		(skin)

D.   Written and Aural Presentation: Combined Positions

1.	kʰʷ			8.	s̪ʷ	æ̃	
2.	tʰ	pʰ		9.	t˭	k̚	
3.	pʰ	z̥		10.	kʰ	eɪ̄	
4.	ɫ̩			11.	t˭	kʰ	
5.	t̚			12.	ɫ̩		
6.	ɫ			13.	kʰ	æ̃	tʰ
7.	ŋ̩			14.	pʰ	ɫ	
				15.	t˭	ī	kʰ

E. Written and Aural Presentation: Combined Positions—Whole Words

1.   m   ʌ   s   ɬ̩

2.   kʰ   æ̃   m   pʰ

3.   s   t˭   õʊ̃   n

4.   l   ʌ   ɣ̥

5.   s̫   w   ī   m

6.   s   p˭   ū   n

7.   θ   ī   ŋ   kʰ

8.   k̫ʰ   w   ɪ   ɬ   tʰ

9.   pʰ   ɔɪ   z̦

10.   s   p˭   ɑ   r   k˭   ɬ̩

F. Aural Only Presentation: Combined Positions—Whole Words (With Spaces)

Real words

1. pʰ   ī   n   ɬ̩

2. s   k˭   æ   n   d   ɬ̩

3. w   ɪ   d̦̩   θ

4. ɪ   s   p˭   aʊ   z̦   d̦

5. m   ɛ   d   ɬ̩

6. k̫ʰ   w   ī   n   z̦

7. d   ʌ   z   ŋ̩   tʰ

8. s   m   oʊ   ɬ   d   ɚ

9. f   æ   n   tʰ   æ   s   t˭   ɪ   k̚

10. s̫   w   ɪ   tʃ

Nonsense words

11. pʰ   l   āɪ   n   tʰ

14. k̫ʰ   w   i   pʰ

12. ɪ   s   p˭   i   t̚

15. ə   b   oʊ   z̦

13. f   æ   n   ɬ̩

16. d   e   t̪̩   θ

G.   Aural Only Presentation: Combined Positions—Whole Words (Without Spaces)

Real words

1.   [fæsn̥d̥]

2.   [hoʊɫdɚ]

3.   [tʰɛ̃n̪ɵ]

4.   [pʰæn̩ɬ]

5.   [hɪdn̩]

6.   [ɪsk⁼epʼ]

7.   [s̥wĩndɬ̩]

8.   [sp⁼æ̃ŋgɬd̥]

9.   [bɪtʰ̫wĩn]

10. [pʰʌdɬ]

Nonsense words

11. [əbeẓ]

12. [kʰ̫wætʰ]

13. [tʰrĩmpʰ]

14. [sɛd̪ɵ]

15. [bĩn̩ɬ]

16. [ɛst⁼epʼ]

Answers: Laboratory Session 7
Suprasegmentals

STRESS

III. Practice Exercises

A. Two-Syllable Words: One Stress

1. sófa
2. assúme
3. cárry
4. allów
5. alígn
6. ínstant
7. yóuthful
8. subdúe
9. destróy
10. mínor
11. diseáse
12. plácard

B. Two-Syllable Words: Two Stresses

1. pòstpóne
2. cónvìct
3. ózòne
4. bláckòut
5. yòursélf
6. stórehòuse
7. sìxteén
8. drúgstòre
9. hìmsélf
10. íncline

C. Three-Syllable Words: One Stress

1. émphasis
2. enjóyment
3. evíction
4. abándon
5. vígilance
6. delícious
7. distínguish
8. émptiness
9. famíliar
10. símilar

D. Three-Syllable Words: Two Stresses

1.	ùnderstánd	6.	mágnifỳ
2.	wéather vàne	7.	èntertáin
3.	òverlóok	8.	mémorìze
4.	sácrifìce	9.	óvercòat
5.	ìntrodúce	10.	èvermóre

E. Four-Syllable Words

1.	sìtuátion	6.	negótiable
2.	dèmolítion	7.	demócracy
3.	philósophy	8.	ámicably
4.	chàrismátic	9.	scìentífic
5.	cònflagrátion	10.	addítional

F. Five-Syllable Words

1.	philosóphical	6.	bìológical
2.	hỳpocrítical	7.	appròpriátion
3.	pronùnciátion	8.	àntithétical
4.	delìberátion	9.	hòmogéneous
5.	nàtionálity	10.	ìnsurmóuntable

G. Final Exercise: Word Stress

1.	blácktòp	7.	lócàte
2.	dánger	8.	constrúct
3.	sánity	9.	destróyer
4.	fríendlier	10.	diréction
5.	catástrophe	11.	ègocéntric
6.	zòológical	12.	appròpriátion

INTONATION

A.   Statements and Wh-Questions

1.	Where's the bús?	B
2.	Í did.	A
3.	You should gét it.	A
4.	It was éarly.	A
5.	He was láte.	B
6.	Who's the ówner?	A
7.	Where is my cóat?	B

B.   Wh-Questions and Yes-No Questions

1.	Which man is your fáther?	B
2.	Who just came ín?	C
3.	Is that Súsan?	A
4.	Have you met Bób?	A
5.	How ís she?	B
6.	Who is thát?	C

Final Exercise: Intonation

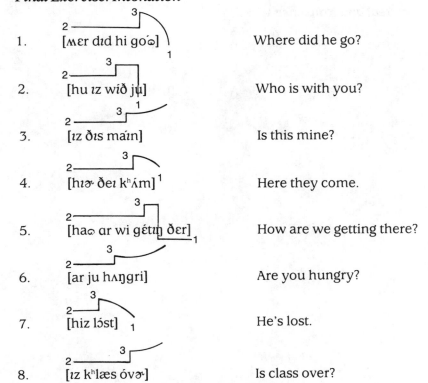

1.   [ʌɛr dɪd hi goʊ]   Where did he go?

2.   [hu ɪz wɪð ju]   Who is with you?

3.   [ɪz ðɪs maɪn]   Is this mine?

4.   [hɪɚ ðeɪ kʰʌm]   Here they come.

5.   [haʊ ɑr wi gétɪŋ ðɛr]   How are we getting there?

6.   [ɑr ju hʌŋgri]   Are you hungry?

7.   [hiz lóst]   He's lost.

8.   [ɪz kʰlæs óvɚ]   Is class over?

LENGTH

A. Length Discrimination

1.	bead	4.	kiss
2.	sued	5.	bug
3.	Madge	6.	maid

B. Written and Aural Presentation: Real Words

1.	bit	*bid*	[bɪːd]	5.	*log*	lock	[lɑːg]
2.	*faze*	face	[feːɪz]	6.	mat	*mass*	[mæːs]
3.	mop	*mob*	[mɔːb]	7.	"H"	*age*	[eːɪdʒ]
4.	moot	*moose*	[muːs]	8.	Bert	*bird*	[bɝːd]

C. Written and Aural Presentation: Nonsense Words

1.	B	/tuli/	/tuːli/	5.	A	/beːne/	/bene/
2.	B	/molo/	/molːo/	6.	A	/suːmə/	/sumə/
3.	B	/gato/	/gɑːto/	7.	B	/taso/	/tɑːso/
4.	A	/bɝˑːle/	/bɝˑle/	8.	B	/sove/	/soːve/

D. Aural Only Presentation: Real and Nonsense Words

1.	B	[noːɞz]	4.	B	[eːte]
2.	A	[meːɪz]	5.	B	[sæːno]
3.	B	[broːɞg]	6.	A	[bʌːlə]

Answers: Laboratory Review III
Consonants, Vowels, Diphthongs, and Diacritics

PRACTICE EXERCISE

Real words

1.	[beɪʒ]	(beige)	9.	[tʃɑ́rmĩŋ]	(charming)
2.	[wɪḓə]	(width)	10.	[dɪstˈróɪ]	(destroy)
3.	[əráɪẓ]	(arise)	11.	[rɪfjúzɬ]	(refusal)
4.	[kʰ̥ʊ́ʃə̃n]	(cushion)	12.	[tʰúəbrʌʃ]	(toothbrush)
5.	[hǽzn̩tʰ]	(hasn't)	13.	[tʰéləfõʊ̃n]	(telephone)
6.	[ṭʰ̥wĩndʒ]	(twinge)	14.	[ɛ̀nɚdʒétˈɪkˀ]	(energetic)
7.	[pʰlǽŋkʰ]	(plank)	15.	[ɛ̀fɚvésə̃ntʰ]	(effervescent)
8.	[òvɚnáɪtʰ]	(overnight)	16.	[ĩnɪskˈépəbli]	(inescapably)

Nonsense words

17.	[mɑ́ʊʒɚ]		21.	[dɔ́bɛ̀ʒ]
18.	[biṱə]		22.	[ʍéndrif]
19.	[gɝ́ðĩŋ]		23.	[gɛ̀fjúdʒɪtʰ]
20.	[ṭʰ̥wīntʰ]		24.	[bəhɑ́ɵrɔitʃ]

Appendix A
Major Parts of the Vocal Tract

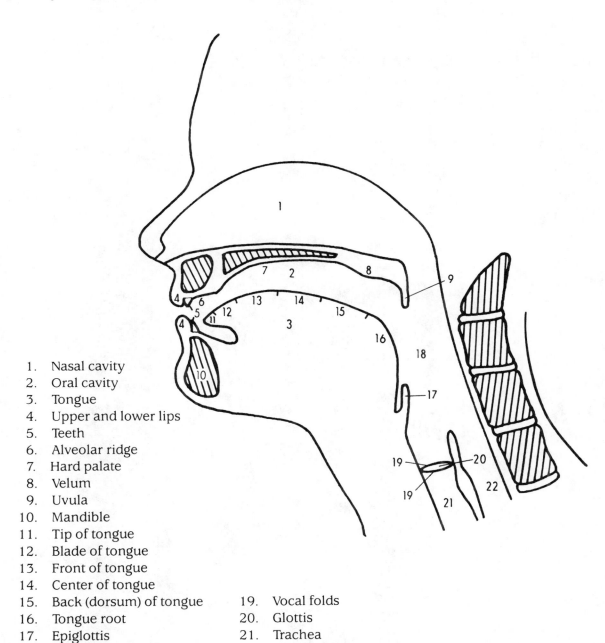

1. Nasal cavity
2. Oral cavity
3. Tongue
4. Upper and lower lips
5. Teeth
6. Alveolar ridge
7. Hard palate
8. Velum
9. Uvula
10. Mandible
11. Tip of tongue
12. Blade of tongue
13. Front of tongue
14. Center of tongue
15. Back (dorsum) of tongue
16. Tongue root
17. Epiglottis
18. Pharynx
19. Vocal folds
20. Glottis
21. Trachea
22. Esophagus

Adapted from P. Ladefoged (1975). *A course in phonetics*. New York: Harcourt Brace Jovanovich.

Appendix B
Points of Articulation

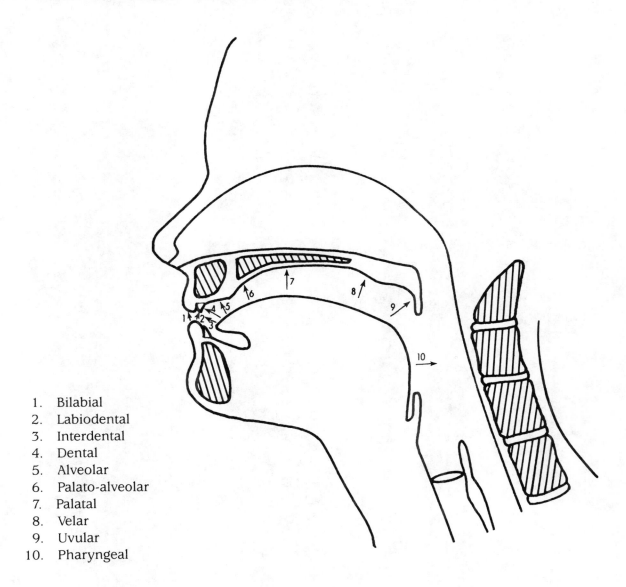

1. Bilabial
2. Labiodental
3. Interdental
4. Dental
5. Alveolar
6. Palato-alveolar
7. Palatal
8. Velar
9. Uvular
10. Pharyngeal

Adapted from P. Ladefoged (1975). *A course in phonetics.* New York: Harcourt Brace Jovanovich.

Appendix C
English Consonants

Point of Articulation

←voiceless voiced→ *	Bilabial	Labio-dental	Inter-dental	Alveolar	Palato-alveolar	Palatal	Velar	Glottal
Stop	p b			t d			k g	
Nasal	m			n			ŋ	
Affricate					tʃ dʒ			
Fricative		f v	θ ð	s z	ʃ ʒ			h
Liquid				l	r			
Glide	ʍ w					j	(ʍ) (w)	

Manner of Articulation

*When symbols for 2 sounds appear in one cell, the sound on the left is voiceless and the one to the right is voiced.

Appendix D
English Vowels

ENGLISH VOWELS

Tongue Position

	Front	Central	Back	
High	i		u	Closed
	ɪ		ʊ	
Mid	e	ɚ ɝ ə	o	Mid / Jaw Position
	ɛ	ʌ	ɔ	
Low	æ a		ɑ	Open
	Spread		Rounded	

Tongue Height

Lips

Appendix E
English Diphthongs

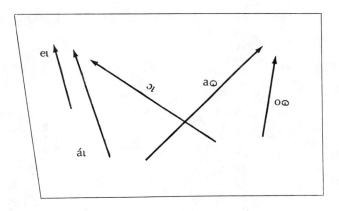

Appendix F
Additional Symbols and Diacritics

[x]	voiceless velar fricative, as in *Bach*
[ɸ]	voiceless bilabial fricative
[β]	voiced bilabial fricative
[ɬ]	voiceless lateral fricative
[pf]	voiceless labial affricate
[ts]	voiceless alveolar affricate
[dz]	voiced alveolar affricate
[ʔ]	glottal stop, as in [mʌʔi]

Stop Release Diacritics

[ʰ]	aspirated, as in [tʰap]
[⁼]	unaspirated, as in [p⁼un]
[˺]	unreleased, as in [kʰæt˺]
[ʻ]	slightly aspirated

Diacritics for Lip Shape

[ʷ]	labialized, as in [s̫wit]
[↔]	protruded labialized
[ʍ] or [ₒ]	unrounded
[⨯]	produced with lip inversion
[ɔ]	a vowel produced with lip rounding
[ᴄ]	a vowel produced with less lip rounding than usual

The additional symbols listed here are part of the International Phonetic Alphabet (1978). Some diacritics are also from the IPA. Others are adapted from Bush and colleagues (1973) and Shriberg and Kent (1982). This is not an exhaustive list of additional symbols and diacritics.

Diacritics for Nasality

[˜]	nasalized, as in [fæ̃n]
[≁]	denasalized
[≈̇]	produced with nasal emission

Diacritics for Length

[:]	lengthened
['] or [˘]	shortened
[ˆ] or [‿]	synchronous

Diacritics for Voicing

[̬]	partially voiced, as in [k̬æt]
[̥]	partially devoiced, as in [spun̥]
[..]	produced with breathy voice (murmured)

Diacritics for Syllabicity

[̩]	a syllabic consonant, as in [bʌtn̩]
[̯]	a nonsyllabic vowel, as in [ðeə̯]

Diacritics for Stress

[´], [ˈ], or [¹]	primary stress
[`], [ˌ], or [²]	secondary stress
[^] or [³]	tertiary (weak) stress

Diacritics for Tongue Position or Shape

[ʲ̦] or [ʲ]	palatalized, as in [sʲu]
[̪]	dentalized, as in [tɛn̪θ]
[~]	velarized, as in [tʰebɫ] (or pharyngealized)
[˞] or [ʳ]	/r/-colored, rhotacized, or retroflexed, as in [kʰa˞]
[ᶜ]or [‿]	lateralized as in [s̮op]
[ᵕ]	markedly grooved
[̼]	produced with a flattened tongue
[_] or [¨]	centralized
[˖] or [→]	retracted tongue, as in [s→op] or [s̠op]
[˗] or [←]	advanced tongue, as in [ʃ← u] or [ʃ̟u]
[⊥] or [^]	raised tongue
[⊤] or [ᵛ]	lowered tongue
[˂]	a fronted sound
[˃]	a backed sound
[̮]	derhotacized or deretroflexed

Other Diacritics

[ˀ], [ʔ], or [̣]	glottalized
[ₓ]	produced with frication
[͎]	whistled
[✓]	trilled

Juncture Markers

+	open juncture
|	internal open juncture
↓	falling terminal juncture
↑	rising terminal juncture
→	checked or held juncture

REFERENCES

Allen, G. (1984). *Transcribing the prosodic (suprasegmental) features of English*. Short course presented at the Annual Convention of the American Speech-Language-Hearing Association, San Francisco, November 17.

Bush, C. N., Edwards, M. L., Luckau, J. M., Stoel, C. M., Macken, M. A., and Petersen, J. D. (1973). *On specifying a system for transcribing consonants in child language: A working paper with examples from American English and Mexican Spanish*. Committee on Linguistics, Stanford University, Stanford, CA.

Chomsky, N., and Halle, M. (1968). *The sound pattern of English*. New York: Harper & Row.

Grate, H. G. (1974). *English pronunciation exercises for Japanese students*. New York: Regents Publishing Company, Inc.

Klein, H. B. (1984). Learning to stress: A case study. *Journal of Child Language, 11*, 375–390.

Ladefoged, P. (1975). *A course in phonetics*. New York: Harcourt Brace Jovanovich.

Lehiste, I. (1970). *Suprasegmentals*. Cambridge, MA: MIT Press.

MacKay, I. (1978). *Introducing practical phonetics*. Boston: Little, Brown and Company.

Pike, K. (1946). *The intonation of American English*. Ann Arbor: University of Michigan Press.

Prator, C. H., and Robinett, B. W. (1972). *Manual of American English pronunciation*. New York: Holt, Rinehart & Winston.

The principles of the International Phonetic Association (1978). London: University College Department of Phonetics.

Shriberg, L. D., and Kent, R. D. (1982). *Clinical phonetics*. New York: John Wiley & Sons.

Smalley, W. A. (1963). *Manual of articulatory phonetics* (revised edition). Tarrytown, NY: Practical Anthropology.